PHIL DUSE EXPOSES:
GOVERNMENT QUACK SILLINESS
TO US "LAW-ABIDING" CITIZENS
(A PEOPLE'S SUIT IS NECESSARY TO CORRECT THIS UNMITIGATED SILLINESS)

A victim of Quack silliness shares the descriptive term that captures Quack no-merit activity:

PROLEPSIS

Meaning: the representation or assumption of a future act or development as if presently existing or accomplished. A Quack mental masturbation process that produces "escaping gas noises" as if the Quack "no-merit" source is disguisable, yet victims need only trust their "noses" to discover "the" true source. Phil's nose knows the truth and shares it here—to support filing of a peoples [victim] suit.

PHILLIP M. DUSE SR.

PUBLISHED BY FIDELI PUBLSIHING INC.

Copyright: 2013 by Phillip M. Duse Sr.

All rights reserved.

No part of this book may be reproduced or transmitted in any form or by any means, electronic or mechanical, including photocopying, recording, or by any information storage and retrieval system, without permission in writing from the copyright owner.

ISBN: 978-1-60414-724-7

To order additional copies of this book, contact: P. Duse by email at philduse@atlanticbb.net or the publisher, Fideli Publishing Inc.

www.FideliPublishing.com

This book was printed in the United States of America.

CONTENTS

Foreword .... *v*

CHAPTER 1
Why Law-Abiders Need this Information 1

CHAPTER 2
Truth Regarding Phil's Background 10

CHAPTER 3
Other Books Written by the Author that Address this Issue 18

CHAPTER 4
First Encounter with Government Professional Liars (DCIS) 25

CHAPTER 5
Specific Instances of Quack Prolepsis Activity 32

CHAPTER 6
Contacts for Purpose of Proving Defamation 40

SIDE BARS
A: Funding the Suit 44
B: Quack Turn-off Button 45
C: The EEOC: "The Real Deal" Not Related to Suit 46
The Scenario that Ignored the Presumed Law 47

ENCLOSURES
First page of relevant documents for initial council review 49

FOREWORD

FIRST: American Law-abiders need to become intimately aware that the bottom line for those being victimized is found under the term "Pestiferous" as in a danger to the US Society—i.e., from sleuthing actions perpetrated by "Quacks" and their ilk to supplant or avoid consequences in US law (such as defamation) or game the system (through ruse and subterfuge).

SECOND: The undeniable bottom line begging action on this issue: "victim(s) currently have no sure-fire legal recourse" Therefore, one must be created from the turmoil of civil litigation—Quacks and their ilk be dammed.

The why and how of the long-standing issues are detailed here with intent to form a basis for victim(s) defamation suit—by utilizing the prolepsis activity itself as the lightning rod to prove defamation—remember Quacks do not have a turn off switch, they apparently believe they are above the consequential and prohibiting defamation laws, they are not!

In reality, Quacks are a mendacious group steeped in "beguile type behaviors." As in rousingly lying and hoodwinking; truth is an option to be avoided or litigated—so let's accept the litigation challenge.

Understanding when Quacks can't contest the merit of the no-merit prolepsis message, they demonize the messenger(s) and their activity has no challenge encounters that compensate victims. Yet, they are the demons who need to be demonized for not having a "truth-based" let alone a worthwhile message to justify their activity—Mental Masturbation (Squeaking Bottom Noises) does not suffice!

Phil brings this message to demonize Quack prolepsis perpetrators and allied messengers to choke them with truths. Yes they will merely continue their sleuthing, that is until they are forced to use the turn off button and pay damages.

Yes for certain they utilize all technology available to them: trailing, planting listening devices and wire taps and in Phil's case even receive a surreptitiously obtained copy of what is printed by his printer: but the truth is still the truth and they just might be caught.

Most important: the quacks and their ilk are actual silliness initiators—their silliness is further explained in this ebook. They engage unwitting and innocent third parties: managers at banks, hotels, resort areas and venders in general. To perpetrate silly entrapments through nefarious ruses staging supposed girly bait scenarios.

Quack ruse staging can only be designed to portend violence of some sort, conjured in their mind, and projected onto their victim (prolepsis) to justify engaging managers, police and or security entities to assist in their initiation of no merit Quack actions through hidden hand subterfuge. The acts, to Phil's knowledge, once conjured in their minds appear to be consistent with a kind of horror fantasies born in demented majority member "Quack & Supporter" mindsets as if only their mindsets represent reality.

The reality is: they perpetrate this activity in spite of no criminality on the part of their target—as it regarded Phil Duse over 28 or more years. Yes, actions of "American" Quacks, to smart for their own intelligence, believing their mental masturbations "replace" reality without possibility of just compensation to their victims-Phil disagrees and will go to the legal mat [he now has sufficient proof] to seek redress and compensation!

CHAPTER 1

WHY LAW-ABIDERS NEED THIS INFORMATION

The historical actions of those in the "Catbird" seat [position of great prominence or advantage] within this US society evolved from a unique adversarial history where they successfully exercised dominion over "all" encountered in whatever area of interest they proclaimed interest in. For example: American Indians, [to say the least] confiscated their land; Mexicans, invaded Mexico in 1848 and confiscated Texas, California, and other areas West of the Mississippi river—a kind of manifest destiny?

With regard to this line of reasoning, I need not get into civil rights related turmoil that spawned "Jim Crow-isms" as mandated policy for certain majority population areas within US localities—that would be unnecessarily technical old school on aberrations no longer at great issue due to overwhelming modern youth acceptance of non racist status quo's. But the point here is: those in the catbird seat of this nation trashed all opponents regardless of propriety or impropriety of their actions as in "my way" or the highway. Propriety could be addressed if at all, after the fact in a manner that upheld or otherwise legalized the catbird intent—dated Supreme Court rulings on rights of some citizens versus other citizens would be classical examples of past catbird no merit social triumphs.

So given this background, it can be stated in its connection with this Book, Prolepsis activity is merely a continuation of unjustifiable actions as if there is was or will be at some later date a justification—well understood by those not in the catbird seat [Women, minorities in general]. Therefore, the issue to be addressed now is when justification is "only" resident in the minds of those in the catbird seat, such as Quacks and their ilk, and not in the laws of the land—the propriety of their actions need to be challenged—to create a turn off button and compensation for victims of the activity.

Today, (2013) laws are not as easily ignored or just set aside [with the exception of EEOC (Equal Employment Opportunity Commission) rules]; today there can be an assignment of fault and/or payment for damage—in spite of the subterfuge hidden hand of majority member catbirds whose numbers are diminishing to suggest a different future is at hand c. 2020—2040.

Remember, the number of catbird seats held by the majority will soon change from the majority to minorities who will actuality believe in and mandate their rights, as stated in the US Constitution and not in mythological "justification by Mental Masturbation", which is the unique Quack "Pestiferous" [danger to minorities in the US society] process not in laws of the land. This change in numbers is a coming reality for the American way, those currently in the catbird seat need to be introduced to the coming reality as quickly as possible, to ensure future cat birders adherence to laws of the land and to cease actions perpetrated because of numbers of backward thinking believers [Quacks and their ilk] that to often ignore, through subterfuge, rights of people victimized by "Prolepsis" activity, minority law-abiders have rights too.

QUESTIONS

Who are the victims you ask?

(1) If you have submitted a complaint to the EEOC for adjudication you discovered that the process in the vast majority of instances does not

result in upholding the complainant's presumed grievance or rights. As proven by the fact that 80% to 90% or more of aggrieved persons filing complaints lose and have been losing for decades. Why is this result a reality? Upon review you discover decisions turn on invented reasoning grounded in what are termed "Agency Articulations" and not proven facts, plus the articulations are not challengeable before the decision is rendered! There are no corresponding "aggrieved person" articulations that carry equal or any weight of consequence in the final EEOC decision process.

The next resulting/consequence for the complainant [persons filing complaint] is the experiences that begin the "Kill the messenger process" which opens the door to Quacks and their ilk to engage demonization and entrap scenarios because the complainer can now be viewed as a false claimant based on the EEOC decision on the claim—in spite of the slanted therefore no justice process. Further legal action is unlikely to change the decision to correct the EEOC slanted process—that's the way the process was designed, apparently, complainants should accept this and forego legalisms/challenges as this is a sad reality. Complainants (all seeking adjudication through the EEOC) are advised to save their legal dollars—fund this suit because—it's the process stupid.

(2) The Example: If you are a minority Government employee and in the course of your official duties you refer an allegation of contractual based impropriety [as in a verbal threat] to the DCIS (Defense Criminal Investigating Service) and they promised to look into the issue, to correct a non minority government employee or essentially any individual who voiced an intent of harm or threat against you! Be advised that person need only allege you are or can be deemed to be a "disgruntled malcontent" who needs to be taught the lesson that your job responsibilities and/or the grievance process, in any regard, is not designed to protect you and indeed will seek to harm you? (See chapter 4) DCIS in all probably will not (did not in Phil's case) correct the non minority who voiced a threat to harm him—they merely ignored the easily provable allegation—this was the first instance in which Phil learned DCIS would not investigate

(as promised) a threat to harm him for merely doing his job. The threat tabled, as later events indicate, was carried out—by prolepsis activity.

This appears to be the case with the possible exception of your having incontrovertible proof of the claim i.e., video or other recording of the incident and if you don't it can not otherwise be assumed or presumed to be a valid complaint (except in the Army where right holds sway over wrong in the overwhelming number of instances)—in a civilian work environment, typically, Prolepsis activity can and did follow. You must also note that most government employees do not carry video or other recording devices in the normal course of discussions with majority members. If the DCIS is involved you probably should if you have a threat based safety concern as the truth is subjective.

(3) An upper level DOD manager or any non minority manager [if you are being demonized] can feign your contemplation of an act of violence or communicate a presumed intent (based of your presence alone) to harm a non minority in spite of there being absolutely no qualifying incident—because you were demonized—qualifying events are communicated in other Phil Duse books. If you are a minority, anticipate a non minority female ruse encounter, directed by a Quack or a Quack resource, Phil's experience, they approach you and stand by exhibiting a silly fake smile (called smiling faker in Phil's books/experience)—Phil typically either ignored them or placed more distance between the ruse female and himself. On aircraft he typically went to sleep.

Note that Quacks and their resources are quite adept at creating ruse scenarios where you haven't a clue, initially, that you are being/have been set up for a negative outcome requiring involvement of police (DCIS/AFOSI/Local security force) Phil's experience—as in a coin flip where heads they win tails you lose. Again, prolepsis activity, your life will never be the same as a result of no merit continuous "Prolepsis" activity. Thus we need a turn off button for victims and defamation compensation!

(4) Remember, the term "Mental Masturbation" it belies the prolepsis concept as a basis to engage third parties as participants in a kind of

"capture a presumed bad guy ruse" of interest to all law-abiders because Quacks, through their demonization process can cause third parties to assume they are "doing the right thing" out of pure ignorance of the underlying reasoning not being truth based therefore not lawful as a fact based capture exercise. It is actions for and by liars personified—Phil Duse experiences.

In general, third parties are not sufficiently aware of the true or underlying reasoning and tend to react to assist Quacks because "historically" that's just the way it is done when dealing with "presumed criminals" and criminality in general. It is apparent Quacks believe if you are a minority you have an enhanced propensity to engage in unlawful actions—because of your minority status alone; that quite frankly is pure bull.

Phil's suit will exclude unwitting third parties even though they may be the party at risk for liability—they are innocent—because the Quacks are playing a hidden hand to absolve themselves of fault—again it's the process stupid don't become a victim of Quack (we are so smart) silliness where they assume you and not them are criminal.

(5) For certain, you are the (American) person you represent to others who you interface with, good, bad, ugly or non committal in terms of demonstrating an observable or tag able behavioral trait that reasonable persons can properly interpret you to be a [negative/positive] American. Conversely, you are not the negative person others may conjure in their mind based on their or local long-standing negative beliefs or historical stereotypes or other personality criteria not otherwise in evidence, that is, to reasonably knowledgeable American persons—meaning if the shoe does not fit don't try to force it.

Non-Americans have unique beliefs that they can compare you with too, again, that is not automatically who you are it is how you are perceived by persons from that non-American society—good, bad, desirable, undesirable etc. But in general just being an American (Phil's experience traveling the world) is a positive based on presumed traits regarding higher income and history of engaging in worthwhile positive endeavors supporting democratic kinds of freedom of mind and spirit—most foreign nationals do not view you as an ugly American unless the assumption has been earned by your instant conduct! (Or their society practices/preaches a preference to dislike Americans.)

The issue in this book: Quacks (in spite of their we're so smart persona) don't' appear to properly consider influences on ones personhood, in particular world traveled professional soldiers who could routinely copulate overseas as well as in the states with females of all hues—in spite of American race issues—typical military socializing does not/has not supported Quack based racism in decades. It is obvious that exclusionary cultural logic on the part of Quacks originate from restrictions in American experiences that at one time were part and parcel to typical quasi American behaviors—as portrayed by Quack entrapment scenarios based on locality or cultural origin—definable here as "old school" southern lifestyle assumptions.

These out dated kinds of beliefs are obviously "bed rock" resident in typical Quack prolepsis activity, to suggest propensity by race [and exclude professional training /experience/cultural environment] where they tend to assign certain negative social behaviors or cognitive limitations not otherwise in fact. Limitations attributable to Quacks fighting personnel demons: fear of minorities, in addition to passé beliefs no longer held by knowledgeable non raciest persons who hold truths to be truth.

For example: this minority (Phil is the example here) had/has to continually attempt to remove him self from involvement with obviously false smiling faker opportunities to copulate with majority member, unattractive or attractive, females who ruse suggest or otherwise presume interest on his part in copulating/dating them—such interest did not exist in the most recent 35 years!

Unfortunately, Quack primary efforts involve continual staging's that are just plain silly in this regard—as the outcomes prove—he never took the bait. The falseness of the fake opportunity appear to be resident in long passé social behaviors of some American females; that no longer exist in the broader population (even Gerry Springer TV guests can attest to this reality) nor does it exist in European females or non American females in general—yet it is particularly resident in Quack ruse actions and mindsets.

Poor things, this is a significant cognitive shortcoming that meant they could not be successful staging this kind of silliness to entrap Phil Duse, who already fulfilled his copulation desires in enormous numbers with females of all hues all over the world.

Quacks don't seam to understand the reality (as stated above) that is part and parcel to professional (certainly Army) solders traveling the world let alone considering the ever present cognitive issues of STD's [sexually transmitted disease] and professional morality—Phil has not been an active or otherwise participant in skirt chasing [as stated above] for more than 35 years. For certain, Quack cognitive shortcoming on this issue is their problem not Phil's. Phil evolved from maturing in the military professional environment and not from civilian ghetto life styles—that Quacks can claim familiarity with. Prolepsis activity on the part of Quacks does not change this reality but is a clear indication of Quack stupidity—in spite of their "we're so smart persona".

(6) Bottom line: Prolepsis activity engages a paradigm change in acceptable social order/logic whereby Quacks, through a hidden hand, bring in "Mental Masturbations" as sufficient justification (not law) to engage in demonization activities against primarily minorities—such as the positive professional minded Phil Duse—without the prospect of being held for defamation damages. This paradigm change instituted by Quacks replace reality with their bias belief system (not based on truths) as if they are empowered by the US legal system, in deed societies in general, to redefine law abiding citizens in the negative, or otherwise according to Quack notions of appropriate cultural actions that simply are not in accordance with existing laws of this land—they are neither Gods nor God like they have the same typical faults as other similarly educated Americans!

Quack actions, though, by default define and address the long standing societal "hidden issue" of: things minorities have to do to stay out of trouble. Essentially accept what is given to them gratis and not what is guaranteed by the Constitution—really now. Therefore, a corrective action by "we the people" including minorities is necessary. It is coming, stay tuned.

AGAIN BECAUSE THERE IS NO TURN-OFF BUTTON!

Classic, more recent, examples of Quack prolepsis activity: occurring in 2013. Phil and his spouse went on a four day vacation to the sunny Bahamas in February. He discovered on the first day of his arrival the Quack prolepsis logic had followed; a Bahaman police person singled him out in the hotel complex to ask seemingly inappropriate questions regarding his vacationing suggesting he was their for some other "unknown activity"? Now who would you think engaged in the demonization of Phil to bring about the inappropriate questioning of the Bahaman police entity—how about U.S. Quacks—what are they trying to prove here?

Why are they continually trying to prove or suggest a probability of criminal behavior to third parties essentially everywhere Phil travels at home and abroad? Behavior as it regards Phil that never existed? And what is the supposed criminal behavior? There are methods (for example Polygraphs/FMRI—Functional Magnetic Resonance Imaging) to rule in or rule out whatever criminal behavior is suspected. If not utilized or even if it is we go direct to the issue of defamation based on the results—Phil is straining at the lease to go to the legal mat to resolve this issue. Again, Phil needs a turn off button and compensation for the activity occurring over a 28-year period, now in two countries (and on a cruise ship too, in 2003)!

Also of interest to the issues, the Bahaman people interfacing with Phil and his wife did so without the animosity brought about or experienced during typical "American" Quack ruse intervention behaviors: at casinos and similar outlets where people come to relax, socialize, and/or engage in legal gaming activities without an alarm expectation of being harmed by unknown third parties let alone Quack directed resources. Fortunately for the vacation enjoyment, Bahamians in general communicating friendliness spoke and gave helpful guidance every where Phil and his spouse went, which made the overall vacation experience truly enlightening and memorable.

At the other extreme, when Quack resources presented "herself" (at least 3 occasions) it was quite noticeable because she intruded in such an openly obvious manner it suggested she was sent to "force" a communication—of no merit in the casino—while other tourist and Bahamians did not engage in such apparent subterfuge like behaviors and sneered at her behavior—as in that's certainly weird? Yes it was and Phil was in a motorized wheel chair; thinking that would discourage such girly ruse behaviors, no such luck he had been demonized in both countries.

Then on the fourth of July Phil, his spouse, youngest daughter and grandson, vacationed for 2 days at a lovely Casino resort complex in Maryland, just South of Pennsylvania. Although he fully expected to experience ruse girly encounters of some sort, the actual encounter had a new twist. Inimical of the child psych game played by his daughter with her son—she would feign giving him something and then say "psych" when he tried to receive it. At this resort, on two occasions, a lady and man and another lady in the hotel hallway gave a gratuitous greeting but before I could respond in kind both parties turned and walked quickly away similar in action to the above psych example. A new Quack ruse is Phil's thought I hope they had fun—next time Phil will ignore them.

CHAPTER 2

TRUTH REGARDING PHIL'S BACKGROUND

Phil Duse currently as well as in yesterdays is among the proudest if not "the" proudest of Black Males in the United States of America. Arguably the greatest Country on the planet where all who work hard [within the rules] to achieve worthwhile goals could be assured or at least assume expectations of successful outcomes equal to their input. Yet Phil discovered, some 28 years ago that, as a result of "out of the blue" surreptitious surveillance and lifestyle disruption activity, unknown "civilian" dolts (a wholly appropriate descriptive demarcation based on the reality) who "obviously" did not know him or had otherwise interfaced with him nevertheless were engaging in menacing ridiculous efforts to present him to his peers in the opposite view of the proud person his life works and professional accomplishments commanded, no he was not an angel—although close to one and certainly not a criminal—just a competent logistical trained hard worker and family man.

The then unknowns acted, as if, Phil should be demonized and dammed because dolts and/or Quack personas supported such an outcome! Really now, dammed for what becomes the million dollar question—to be answered by defamation suit? Could the reason be because he was immanently successful in lawful life pursuits; Marriage [48 years and counting, no debts] and raising and educating the 3 kids he had with his wife? Or because he was assigned high quality security defined jobs in the military: Responsible for the receipt storage and issue of all narcotics and precious metals issued to Madigan Army Medical Center for consumption in the four states of: Washington, Montana, Oregon and Idaho. Or for the civilian jobs he held? [See chapter 4.]

If due to his financial security, which is the result of having the wisdom to save a portion of his income over decades (as in: in order to have money when you want it don't spend all of it when you get it) and doing so consistently in spite of historical cognitive pitfalls on this issue by a significant percentage of Americans his age in general. Yes, such reasoning is logical—to Phil at least—and responsible for his modicum of success.

Or is the demonization of Phil for not tap dancing on command under the notion of "Things minorities have to do in order to stay out of trouble?" Or other similar past U.S. society demeaning understandings more unique to minorities than non-minorities? Here defined as typical historical actions that once outright prevented minorities/females from achieving a higher rung on latter's leading to success or otherwise higher achievements in comparison to non-minority Americans? That would be the reasoning to Phil. And if so, that's just too bad, Quacks can either like it or lump it! Phil is satisfied with his positive life achievements and Quack prolepsis activity cannot change this reality in spite of their best ruse idiotic and silliness efforts by smiling fakers.

The above comments are the lead in to discuss no merit type actions of those having Quack type degrees and it's effect in regard to demeaning beliefs on propensity for criminality of minorities (logic born in yesteryears probably regarding individuals who were routinely discriminated against by the grater society) still prevalent in significant Quack mindsets based on their permissiveness for prolepsis activity of no merit today. Such mindsets can be properly interpreted to suggest they tend to view themselves as having "God Like" decision powers; remember they continually and wrongly predict never occurring events conjured for support by their metal masturbations. As in the apparent tendency to assign fault based on race—as opposed to lack of resources and or opportunities or plain greed, which can apply to all races in America.

When decision is based on non factual and non existing events, that suggests to normal persons that it is derived from or predicated on a demented core belief system; in any regard, comments are easily supported because their actions are certainly not based on reality as it regards Phil Duse—who as stated—wants to go to the legal mat to secure justice and compensation to prove this point and thereby thwart future no merit activity of this sort!

Actually, as discussed above, examples are presented in this Book because the reality is the actions are "pure" prolepsis lower bottom contemplations in nature; fictional beliefs held to be factual because they "can't" be questioned or challenged, the proper understanding. They soon will be! Because such beliefs can now be compared with real life events of Phil Duse and disqualified on that basis alone—if nothing else the 28 years of their ruse efforts prove Phil's good citizenship—but Quacks keep trying to disprove this reality as if their mindsets represent reality and not reality it self.

Phil can withstand any and all claims of no true merit: girly ruses being the dominant thrust of their prolepsis activity along with disapproval of high quality jobs managers assigned to Phil! Again as stated previously to test claims of criminality why not utilize available technology—Polygraphs, Functional Magnetic Resonance Imaging FMRI—and then let the results speak for Quack claims versus reality. Phil intends to feed them "actual" truths that Quacks and their ilk can dissect to see if they fit under their prolepsis claims and or criminality beliefs and if it does not we can then discuss, at trial, issues of defamation and compensation—to achieve a proper closure on the issues.

Yes it is understood that Quacks and those supporting their efforts will merely deny their involvement and refuse to divulge their 28 years of record accumulation proving prolepsis and job intrusion activity—but we know the proof exist—owing to past EEOC adjudications. As do some of the "managers" and others too, conscripted by Quacks and their ilk, to assist in their no merit efforts; this is a reality that just might be their down fall and lead to a turn off button—with compensation.

This is but one cognitive reality omitted from their prolepsis activity that introduced great reputational, financial and defamation harm to victims—such as Phil Duse. When the suit is filed, Quacks have to hope all managers as well as all others—authorizers of the activity—with merit able knowledge on the issues will lie for them, don't they? Phil believes some will spill the beans of truth—to let the cat of truth out of the proverbial prolepsis bag.

Jobs assignments: To further qualify the context of discussions in this Book we differentiate between military mission jobs—in which all jobs are directly/indirectly geared toward defense of the nation—and civilian positions—where a manager hires an employee(s) into a jobs or position primarily defined by "position descriptions" which may be short term in nature as in until a function is complete or long term until the employee retires or the company goes out of business—a general understanding.

In the military (Army) job holders have "Occupational Specialties:" assigned for performance by either an enlisted, warrant officer or commissioned officer placed in the job position. Enlisted personnel undergo job specific training, annual occupational testing and are advanced in rank as they ascend and gain experience in the position to become professional soldiers. Officers undergo specific job related training too but are not necessarily tested every year, their testing is generally more performance based as in demonstration of success in the leadership role or performance in technical areas of an assigned position—logistics and maintenance being the two broad areas in which Phil was trained.

Phil's military jobs were in logistical support areas: medical supply, inventory management, requisitioning materials/equipment from government supply sources such as petroleum, spare parts, even nurse uniforms, to support units he was assigned to: Infantry, Artillery, Warehousing, Engineers (Map Making) and a Nursing College once located on the Walter Reed Army Hospital then located in Washington,

DC. His professional knowledge and people interface skills were derived from experiences working in the aforementioned military environments at home and abroad with military and civilian personnel too—when assigned to hospital environments [Europe/Washington DC and Washington State].

The above discussion is deemed necessary to highlight that at no time in military jobs did he experience unconscious atonable situation similar to that experienced in civilian jobs where unnamed others in the organization "Sea Navy/Air Force/Department of Defense" not his supervisor and without the knowledge of his supervisor, could and did, apparently, instruct NCIS "Navy Criminal Investigating Service personnel and equivalent AFOSI Air Force Office of Special Investigations personnel" to physically (assault) engage Phil Duse—at a contractor plant location in Connecticut and in a California Silicon Valley bar location. Actions to cause Phil bodily harm, certainly life threatening, for his carrying out contractual functions assigned by his supervisor and otherwise obligated by the contractor performing on contracts under his audit function review! Yes there was prolepsis by a Southern Officer, not the norm just typical racism.

With great dismay, Phil discovered that in the Department of Defense entities not in your supervisory chain can cause their police [NCIS/AFOSI] to work in their steed like common street thugs to commit assaults against Phil Duse with apparent immunity; they need only to falsely impute their victim—who had no prior knowledge of being set up—as the instigator! The victim is one person the assaulting individuals were at least three probably armed individuals—how's that for U.S. justice?

To Phil he was performing a contractual job and not a lethal mission with possible life ending consequences inimical of his assignment to the Republic of Vietnam. Phil did not have the slightest idea that he was set up for this kind of deadly outcome on a civilian non-construction job where he, apparently, was so despised by third parties. Parties not in his chain of command that had no involvement with the instant function he was responsible for requiring his presence.

But it happened on two occasions without a possibility of redress or consequence for the perpetrators—similar life threatening incidents occurred over the 28 year period and are discussed in this Book and other Phil Duse books—Why remains to be the unanswered question? Where is the justice for Phil? See chapter 4 for more specific verbal illustrations on the "out of the blue beginning of the hard to fathom questionable activity to harm Phil Duse, the Property Administrator of choice for the supervisors who hired him to carry out audit demands of cognizable/responsible Contracting Officers.

The actions to thwart Phil and or end his existence can only be related to his effectiveness in performing jobs at what is called the "FEBA" in military parlance or "Forward Edge of the Battle Area" dealing with civilian contractors as instructed by his management/contracting officers and authorized by contractual guidance. The job environment difference of note is the reality of the kinds of outrageous harming behavior permitted in spite of its obvious unlawfulness and criminal sanctions under U.S. criminal law.

But in this environment, if a report or complaint was rendered by Phil to DCIS as he had done on a previously occasion, for other than contractor non-compliance with contractual inventory reporting and unauthorized charges to a contract—Phil reported threats to harm him from a Government entity under investigation. Phil discovered such report if not resolved by DCIS [it wasn't] would go by employee obligation to the EEOC, WHY? Phil placed his professional belief in the assurances given by his DCIS contact; but later experiences prove such belief to be pure folly.

Past experiences of Phil clearly indicate the complaint would not and did not receive justice it clearly deserves as a deterrence of consequence under U.S. law. This result is but one reason why, for example as it regards the EEOC's complaint resolution history, the conclusion of merit suggest the typical no justice result is because "it's the system stupid" justice for a complainant is very obvious not the EEOC process goal.

Regarding DCIS: "who knows what drives their sense of justice in spite of their investigative charter; in Phil's experience they supported one side of the equation unrelated to actual empirical fault, when a minority was the initiator of a merit based easily provable complaint, DCIS appeared to help the non minority perpetrator and did not share or otherwise attempt to justify reasoning with the complaint initiator—a type resolution that appears to uniquely apply to American minorities?

QUESTION: How did Phil get his initial Government job?

ANSWER: The first job after retiring from the U.S. Army; he retired on a Friday and went to work for a Civilian Contractor (Bendix Field Engineering, Columbia Maryland) the next Monday. Initially he was hired to work on a contract proposal for operation of the Desert Warfare Training Center being established at Death Valley California. Bendix did not win the contract, unfortunately, and Phil left the company after three or so months to work for a "Head Hunter" company located at Tyson Corners Va.

He was there for only a couple of weeks when Bendix called to inform him they wanted him as a permanent employee and had created a supervisory position in their "Repair and Calibration Laboratory" for him to supervise a six person team engaged in acquiring parts for NASA satellite tracking systems located about every 15 degrees around the planet.

Phil accepted the position and a year later, a Government employee [Property Administrator, Mr. Charlie Keel] who had just reviewed his Bendix operation informed him that the Government need individuals with his proven outstanding logistical skills—comment based on his recent audit. Stating if he agreed he would generate the hiring papers to arrange for his Government employment, the significance is, it was during a Government hiring freeze—Phil agreed—the hiring was arranged through their Columbia Maryland office and Phil was sent to work out of their Silver Springs Md. Office—with a "Motley Crew" of civilian trained Property Administrators with considerable lesser skills—in Phil's view related to minimal relevant training in key logistical area of acquiring material from Government supply sources, Transportation and financing of Government contract work. For example, some government contracts require PA assistance and some don't: they did not appear to understand the differences in PA responsibility of when to investigate loss or damage to government property or not.

Chapter 4 resumes relevant events occurring after Phil's joined the Government: as a Property Administrator (PA) responsible for audits of contractors on the West and South sides of the DC Beltway, he conducted scores of audit over a four year period. Initially of note, for three years, he was the only minority PA in the Silver Springs Md. Office, responsible for contract audit reviews on contractor management of multiple millions of dollars of Government owned property involving scores of DC and Virginia contractors; essentially the same kinds of function performed as a Senior Non Commissioned Officer and S-4 Supply/Warrant Officer in the Military.

He performed essentially the same functions for the Navy Air Systems Command in regards to large air craft and air craft engine manufacturing Contractors—such as Boeing, Westinghouse, Grumman and Sikorsky.

In the next chapter we present the essence of what Phil Duse books covers regarding issues in this book. The purpose is to demonstrate that Phil did all within his powers to seek justice for the out of the blue sleuthing and COTR (Contracting Officer Technical Representative, [COTR is not a Contracting Officer]) threat to harm him. There is a sad reality that justice was not and would not be available to Phil Duse, yet.

CHAPTER 3

OTHER BOOKS WRITTEN BY THE AUTHOR THAT ADDRESS THIS ISSUE

Phil produced multiple books to inform the public of the outrageous events confronted while caring out duties and responsibilities of the positions he was hired into. The entity having or creating the job did so with the expectation of employing Phil Duse to work and resolve the logistical contractual issues that he had proven skills qualifying him to be a consummate expert, one of the best if not the best in the contract logistic/property administration field. For example he was assigned to participate, as the U.S. Navy representative, in the development of a comprehensive contract property control manual for the Department of Defense (DOD)—DOD 4160.2-M.

A interesting comprehensive book by Phil Duse detailing contentious events referred for resolution through investigative efforts of the Equal Employment Opportunity Commission (according to their charter) is:

EEOC: The Real Deal
ISBNs 1-4010-4654-1/4653-3

The cover informs readers to **"Hold your Nose and Discover:"**

1. The author has found them to be "players of low integrity" who permitted an agency to unilaterally alter complaints and misrepresent issues to appear as the "folly of fools."

2. He also believes they assisted others, Department of Justice DOJ, for example, and the District Federal/Appellate Courts in avoiding agency liability for proven violations of Title VII, 1964 Civil Rights Act—how? The complete story in exquisite detail is shared for your edification.

3. Another conclusion of the author holds: They appear to have assisted the U.S. Supreme Court to not rule on the merits of issues, thus denying justice by trial under Title VII!

4. It would appear that they are among the entities who took no action, looked the other way, on a griping report involving actions of "hit men" attempting to terminate the author's life-was the Government involved? See chapter 3. Why? Who else?

THE FOREWORD: The book is a follow-up to the book first published in 1998: *Phil Duse Versus the Tyranny of DOD (Intelligence and Investigative Agencies)*. It includes the promised "Final Chapter" on results of the Civil Suit. Suit number—CA No. 99-1400-A—$10 million in compensatory and punitive damages for pain, suffering and unwarranted sleuthing activity allegedly perpetrated by the government entities depicted in the book. The civil suit was filed in the Fourth District Federal Court, Alexandria VA, and litigated, pro se, through the Fourth District Appellate Court to the U.S. Supreme Court.

As a result of litigating the Civil Suit pro se, the author's knowledge of the suit process increased substantially, particularly as it regards quasi-legalistic sleights of hand available to government defendants in this process brokered by the EEOC. The sleights of hands in the process are exposed under the bright light of the 1st amendment for the public's edification on perceptions of sleuthing by witting and unwitting government entities. The public will learn the "Real Deal" on EEOC tricks and maneuvers in its application of (supposed) remedial remedies under Title VII of the 1964 Civil Rights Act. The author notes that the vast majority of Title VII citizen complaints reflect a reality that complaints referred to the EEOC seldom receive the justice presumed to be available under the act, as proven by statistical results alone. This book explains why this is so.

The next book of interest is the 2004 reprint of the book mentioned above, titled:

(2004: Phil Duse Versus the Tyranny of DOD/DOJ) and its Intelligence and Investigative Agencies—A David Versus Goliath Story
ISBNs 1-4134-5203-5/5202-7.
There is also an ebook of the same title available in all ebook formats.

THE FOREWORD (the first two paragraphs): The story you are about to read is drawn from the harrowing personal experiences of its author, Phillip M. Duse. The story has been revised extensively since its first publication in 1998. This 2004 version improves on the original language and, more importantly, reports ruse evens occurring since 1998. This updated version of events also includes summations and conclusions that clearly bring out the retaliatory nature of Government ruse actions. You will also note that EEOC rules to the contrary are of no practical value as they are too easily undermined and/or ignored by Government obfuscations and its network of ruse perpetrators!

WHY THIS BOOK: To inform America's youth and teachers world wide about how our system of freedom actually works—to expose the illusion of fairness for the fraud that it is. Background: It is not widely known but Mr. Duse is the first black male to have had broad ranging access to top-secret United States Programs dealing with weaponry classified top secret under procurement contracts administered by the former Defense Contract Management Command (DCMC), a former subordinate activity of the Defense Logistics Agency, the starting point of our story that is yet to end.

BACK COVER: This book is directed towards law-abiding people of the Western world, [again] particularly teachers and students. It shares horrific experiences of its author who was forced to deal with and intellectually counter unlawful actions of U.S. Government and local investigative entities. Why? For initiation of EEO complaints alleging improper activity in a top secret contract oversight environment and filing a civil suit exposing the activity, as is our constitutional right.

The next book is titled *False Color of Authority*
ISBN 13: 978-1-4257-3599-9/3598-2.

THE BOOK'S DEDICATION PAGE INFORMS: This book is dedicated to the tens of thousands of individuals (called complainants in EEOC parlance) fooled into referring aggrieved complaints to the EEOC and civil courts, too, believing it would be given unbiased adjudication reference in civil and EEOC statures governing processing of issues alleged to be discriminatory.

Know that you were among a large group certainly fooled into utilizing a process that by evidence of results was fraught with the hidden injustices now made known in this book. The information in this book is for edification of future complaints to prevent continuation of support for unjust judicial processes.

Work to change the existing system through incorporation of latest truth detection technology such as: "Functional Magnetic Resonance Imaging (FMRI): "Brain Fingerprinting" to ensure what defendants falsely claim is detectable by complainants so that the actual truth rules- resulting in true justice.

The back cover sets up the contents of the book: The purpose of this book is to bring long standing false color of authority civil and criminal actions of U.S. government and local entities [we're so smart Quacks and Dolts] to the attention of law abiding people.

THE EXAMPLE: the EEOC's "Equal Employment Opportunity Commission" promises and exploits as they regard enforcing your civil rights. Proven false and exposed as the "actual" justice denying process producing the renowned unfathomable lopsided 90% or more decisions in defendant's favor. If you refer your issue to the EEOC process you should know you are going to lose at the outset, as it is fraught with "injustice-loopholes".

Chapter 3 shares:
"Quackery, Virginia to Pennsylvania, Government hit-men"

In addition to ongoing ruses, chicanery and the like there is another term with direct bearing to the author's umbrella discussion on "false color of authority" by Government and local perpetrators. The term is "Quackery" or decisions by individuals attempting to assist perpetrators through miss reading of mental masturbation conclusions or studies on criminality. They do so, apparently, to derive a semblance of justification for non-empirical based results to apply to law-abiding citizens. Their activity is in support of perpetrators regardless of countervailing facts. The process in its dolt logic use is "a bending of concepts derived through psychological examination or behaviors attributable to non-law-abiders to fit a predetermined preference or outcome for a law-abider—another definition of quackery—as this psychological chicanery concept is not remotely representative of any life reality applicable to the author.

The next book is titled: *US Government Quacks and Dolts (Engaging in Defamation/Entrapments Strategies to get Phil Duse)*

FOREWORD: In this book, 2009 updates and exerts regarding entrapment scenarios and ruse events, initially presented in three books, published by Xlibris, have been consolidated and conclusions drawn by the author, considering events in the three books, are shared in this one comprehensive book. A consolidation of dastardly events of presumably Government Quacks, Dolts and Animosities of every stripe that should prove useful, for edification of readers interested in the events. Such interested parties may not have purchased the other books—this one book will bring all interested parties up to speed—-plus share the new, exciting, patented game of "Three Hand Pinochle" the author is the patent holder—see www.phillipduse.com.

The author strongly suggests there are "Government system gamers" who unduly violate constitutional rights of "Law abiding" citizens as if the constitutional rights are only presumptions in second place to system gamers "mental masturbation" conclusions "easily" provable to either have investigative merit—or not! Conclusions that with current technology—Functional Magnetic Resonance Imaging—can be ruled "wholly" appropriate or "squeaking lower bottom voices" before Law-Abider rights are infringed upon. So far, Government appears to refuse to undertake utilization of the new FMRI technology, so as to ensure it is part and parcel to proper activity of Government—Law-Abiders want to change this apparent reality—and Phil Duse is acting on that belief.

The most recent book before this book is a 2012 e-book published by Fideli titled: *Phil Duse: 25 + Years Combating Ruses*. This book cuts to the chase to define in detail:

RUSES EMPLOYED BY GOVERNMENT QUACKS, TO ILLUSTRATE:

A. Lying is their core expertise. Truths are mere opinions.

B. Goal: fool the public to help them harm the "Messenger."

C. Results: "non racist" Americans are "tricked" to provide Quacks and their ilk undo assistance.

D. Unfortunately, ruses are a "standard American" anomaly honed in yesteryears but still prevalent today—primarily the result of society's non use of "Functional Magnetic Resonance Imaging" Technology [FMRI]. An existing science that will betray a claimed truth from ones mouth, by conclusively showing when the brain disagrees. Quacks and their supporters will be forced into an epiphany on "truths" that replace no merit investigative and psychological ruses.

This book's Chapter 3 shares: Phil Joins Top Secret Organization (A Black James Bond?)

Then Chapter 4: Quacks are Lifestyle Disrupters: IRS Tax Liability Claim (totally false)

Disrupt Casino Gaming; Heretics—Person Dissenting From Religious Doctrine on Head of Household; Phil Duse is the Head of his Household—Quacks be dammed and Black Females Sleuthing?

AND CHAPTER 5: INCLUDES—The Bottom Line; Quack Girly Ruses are Utter Failure. Altoona, PA Chemical Hit Man—to be addressed during suit process? And Phil and his spouse's 2013 Bahaman Vacation.

The above books constitute Phil's detailing of events occurring after the "Out of the Blue" activity of third parties (Civilian Quacks and Dolts) engaging in unfathomable moronic silliness because the activity, presumably, can not be challenged; stay tuned a challenge is coming to address what is now known to be "Prolepsis activity "as stated herein.

CHAPTER 4

FIRST ENCOUNTER WITH GOVERNMENT PROFESSIONAL LIARS (DCIS)

Phil Duse, in his professional career in the military and as a civilian, established the performance goal to maximize positive responses to guidance council and direction from the upper echelon/supervisory individuals who hire him and assign responsible task for him to accomplish—in the logistical/contracting field. One creates a positive reputation among upper management echelons by being known to be a knowledgeable, straight talking, high achiever. Such reputation typically morphs into faster promotions and job assignments of ever increasing responsibilities—race in material—Phil is the proof of this reality and received fast track promotions in the military [E-7 at age 27, retired as a Chief Warrant Officer]. And in civilian government jobs [hired at grade 11 promoted to 14] supported by his supervisor/managers had asked for him, as opposed to Phil asking them for the jobs he held.

In a nut shell that has been the reality of Phil's work history sense the age of 24; the exception being when he worked with/for/ individuals who appear unable to function in the more appropriate modern day non-raciest manner; whereby they support logic from yesteryears, denounced in today's society as no longer appropriate for normal thinking people no longer tied to once was or use to bee's.

The problem confronted by Phil, in a general sense, is yesteryear individuals tend to expect Phil to forego what's absolutely right today in order to support what is passé unacceptable to modern normal thinking non-racist persons. That is an issue Phil is aware of but consistently refused to support [yesteryear logic] regardless of who expected it. His life entitlements as a professional minded U.S. citizen are his entitlements and he does not squander them on silliness, fakery and the like—as in what he qualifies to be [amongst other descriptive names] Quack/Dolt/perpetrator's logic—who knowingly or not expect one to work for "Atta boy" like gratuities—really, how about Quacks defining, in writing for third party review, the specifics of how it should be done? Yes that would be defining a form of Jim Crowe/Uncle Tom behavior.

The above understanding is necessary as the qualifying lead into Phil's initial encounter with DCIS agents assigned to investigate contractual mismanagement issues at a contractor location under Phil's Property Administration control. Phil was now the person responsible for correcting property management and accounting issues that had been in a less than appropriate form for a number of years before his arrival. Phil brought about the necessary corrections to the contractor's inventory and accounting postures in accordance with contractual mandates. The last contentious item in this regard was writing off multiple million dollars of inventory not accounted for by inventory results. As a penalty, Phil recommended the contractor be fined/charged 1,000,000 dollars that the contractor could attempt to recover through the government's contractor appeal review board.

He made the above recommendation to his management and they referred the issue to the next managerial level. That level did not support only a one million dollar fine [with holding of contractor payment] and initiated an investigation in which they sought to punish the contractor in criminal [failed] and civil court [failed again]—Phil would be the governments witness on the contract issues regarding audit results indicating contractor liability—the only appropriate remedy from Phil's perspective was the aforementioned $1,000,000 reduction to reimbursements due the contractor.

The investigation brought Phil into contact with several DCIS agents that he provided whatever information available to him as they requested. The issue: Phil perspective held he was doing his standard job when providing assistance asked for by the DCIS agents. But, Phil discovered the DCIS agents (one in particular) was not only not truthful in dealing regarding the contractor but actually miss-lead him to believe the contractor was in cahoots with or the initiator of then unknown individuals who he reported appeared "out of the blue" to follow and disrupt his social activities in local Army Officer Clubs and other venues he visited!

Phil had no prior experience dealing with these kinds of investigator mindsets and [unfortunately] did not realize he was being fooled until years later; when he discovered two of the girls engaged in Officer Club sleuthing in fact worked for/with this DCIS agent that had been lying to him for years. Not knowing/perceiving the deceit nature of the interface, Phil often accompanied the DCIS agent on visits to offices of government prosecutors who also never let Phil in on the "real deal" behind the ongoing sleuthing activities: leaving Phil to believe the contractor was responsible when said contractor played no part in the sleuthing whatsoever—what were the Quacks trying to accomplish?

The lie: they told Phil in addition to investigating the contractor they were also investigating the issue he reported about being threatened by a government employee and, more importantly, he should not otherwise involve himself any further in the issue as it would interfere with their investigation—in hindsight they appear to have been protecting the COTR? At the time Phil, out of ignorance, believed the folly to his peril.

A COTR "Contracting Officer Technical Representative" had threatened Phil over the phone: "Were going to get you" he said! Phil wondered for what at the time because he had resolved all of the contract property accounting issues! To resolve the threat issue, he initially referred it to his management who arranged for a meeting with COTR management but no one came? Unfortunately, Phil could not carry out his intent to personally confront the COTR because, as stated, the DCIS agent prohibited any contact—again when viewed in hind sight—

logically the no contact instruction possibly/apparently permitted resulting prolepsis activity or other retaliatory action at the behest of COTRs? (No justice for Phil—a American sleuthing reality)

He later learned the COTR at issue did not agree with Phil forcing them to follow contract rules regarding removing inventory from the "parts depot" without proper paperwork. They [individuals sent by COTRs] were accustomed to removing items from the depot without regard to proper paperwork thereby not permitting the contractor to accurately make in and out postings to accounting records. Phil ended the practice and forced them to submit paperwork for what they received from the depot, thus avoiding future inventory accounting issues— because that's what the contract required—not Phil. Failure to do so during Phil's watch would/could be interpreted to mean Phil would be responsible for future improper audit/inventory related issues—that was not going to happen on his watch.

There was an additional contentious accounting issue uncovered by Phil, it involved contractor charges (400 million) to contracts that did not have an active/current authorization to receive the charges— the charges were booked during one cycle and dropped during the next (called kiting). The contractor had to reverse charges to the government accounts to their own. Again Phil audit action was instrumental in identifying the inappropriate charges: but he could not collect a percent of money saved (under Qui tan provisions) because the information, according to the reviewing authority, was part and parcel to his expected job performance. He got only a performance award of $1,500 or so.

BOTTOM LINE: lying by DCIS agents opened a new learning curve for Phil as, professionally, he engaged in only disciplined responses based on the reality of the issue at hand and never lying for the pure sake of lying to hide known truths—which he discovered was the major thrust of DCIS activity. He now understands more clearly that "civilian" [as opposed to military environment] communications appear to often have a problematic component that is not based on sound reasoning related to the mission or responsibilities of the person they are engaging—such logic is of little use to professional merit based thinking—appears to be based on psychology of deceit regardless of subject.

It is as if they are culturally unable to realize or unconditionally accept sound professional responses [from a professional doing his job] void of cultural proclivities and bias. Or so it seems: when dealing with a professional minority such as Phil! That is uniquely their problem as it was not Phil who engaged in subterfuge and lying to protect the contractor or any one else involved with the issues at hand. But in hindsight, prolepsis activity became the resultant reality of the interface, driven by their apparent culturally definable "Mental Masturbation" beliefs of no true merit.

This aforementioned logic [again in hindsight] opens the door for preconceived behaviors based on U.S. cultural proclivities or perceptions [unique American raciest logic] with a strong yesteryear leaning predicated on locality, North, South etc. ... As opposed to empirical facts. Had Phil known of this DCIS logic shortcoming up-front [they would disagree] he would have pursued addressing the COTR threat directly with the COTR in addition to his manager to force a resolution one way or the other and not engage or otherwise deal with DCIS lying for their own posterity, as if lying could resolve the issues.

Their lies should be their problem and not his. Phil was doing the Property Administrator job as expected and does not deal with unprofessional foolishness unrelated to his job responsibilities. Therefore, based on the continuation of ruses at this decades-later stage of sleuthing activity, it is clear to Phil his professional qualities are viewed as if they are nonexistent or "viewed from a civilian yesteryear standpoint" don't apply because Quacks disagree with the reality. Really now—lets go to the mat and see who should be disbelieved!

Learning Curve information that stood the test of time: Civilian mindsets sent young civilian white females into officer clubs to engage in sleuthing under a belief or intent to entice Black officers and Phil associates to? The logic, what ever it is, was not smart/appropriate because (1) by their street like behavior they had no knowledge of proper "Officer" social interfaces. (2) They had not been invited by any member of the group they were trying to infiltrate–inimical of either a bad European spy movie or street walkers wanting to make a sale. (3) Were beyond silly: as by their smiling they actually expected the officers to accept their presence just because they positioned themselves among the social group—they were by and large ignored.

The person who sent them is a "civilian/knowledge trained" American idiot who did not know the behavior might be appropriate for an enlisted men's club but certainly not an Officer's club. Their ruse sleuthing actions and who ever sent them suggest they believed their "presence" alone would be sufficient to gain social entry into the group of active duty and retired Army military officers; worldly experienced comrades Phil Duse socialized with.

Apparently the DCIS sender(s) believed Black officers had no expectation of appropriate social behavior beyond what can be generally expected of a venue for enlisted soldiers, NCO and Enlisted men's clubs; a significant cognitive shortcoming. Phil states this here because hindsight indicates this was the basic sleuthing behavior /style perpetrated by Quacks and their ilk during literally 1000s of ruse encounters occurring over 28 or more years—Quacks attempting to replace Phil's reality with their mental masturbation beliefs as if such beliefs represented reality. Such beliefs are factually and practically impossible to depict truths when only predicated on American "civilian" logic as if it also applies to worldly experienced professional soldiers with much broader life experiences to draw from.

The ultimate effect of the no merit ruse encounters interfered with Phil's social and professional life. Quack persistent demonization of his good name changed/retarded Phil's ability to communicate with and or build normal friendships as whoever he communicated with more likely than not would be conscripted to help Quack initiatives—an American prolepsis reality—available for exclusive use by Quacks and their ilk gaming the U.S. legal system.

Essentially every venue Phil patronized/visited since the initial "out of the blue" activity was encumbered by ruse perpetrators (White, Black, male, female) making their no value intrusion intents know through rank silliness, i.e., smiling, nonsense conversational attempts—also called attempted entrapments and **Defamation**—as it regards demonization of Phil involving innocent third parties/managers of the venues he visits.

Quacks are not above the laws and should be held liable as the bottom line of their activity constitutes unabashed no merit prolepsis activity to harm and or entrap Phil [and others similarly situated] who had no possible recourse to stop the activity—or so it seems thus far! Phil wants to be paid for his suffering of prolepsis activity, and create a turn off button for him as well as others being victimized by the no merit activity.

CONCLUSION: The prolepsis activity is a clear indication that Quack intrusions into Phil's life [best example] are or can be considered acts of misguided individuals who are in the final analysis to smart for their own intelligence—and the legal system. The unrelenting nature of the no merit activity suggests the legal system they work for has too much leeway/experience to fund no merit Quack initiatives and or to accept no merit reasoning. Just because Quacks and their ilk say so, in spite of it's lacking a factual reality basis. Therefore they cause undue harm to their target, when the lacking in reality should have been a show-stopper. But, apparently that has not been a problem within the current [and past] American style of lopsided justice!

Hopefully in the not to distant future it will be a rectifiable problem, and end Quack based trashing of ones fourth Amendment Constitutional rights through surreptitious hacking, planting listing devices, following; sleuthing in general as if they are or should be above the laws. The logic behind the activity reminds Phil of the "Agency Articulations" i.e., unproven concepts accepted by the EEOC as fact that become the non factual basis for EEOC grossly faulty conclusions, in favor of defendants, by the often reported 90 or more percent of EEOC cases.

More specifics on these issues are shared in the next chapter and other Phil Duse books.

CHAPTER 5

SPECIFIC INSTANCES OF QUACK PROLEPSIS ACTIVITY

For more than the last quarter century one of the proudest professional Black Males in America, Phil Duse, has been subjected to unrelenting surreptitious silliness of Quacks and their ilk; because he was overwhelmingly successful in the jobs assigned to him by the managers who sought out his professional services—he never asked for the jobs they [Managers of the jobs] asked for him specifically. Every job assigned to him was predicated on his known and proven capabilities and accomplishments in the Logistical/Contract/Property Management field for which he had few equals—this is obviously true because the jobs otherwise would have been assigned to others [read Whites here] with the necessary or similar proven skills.

Yet, the reality of time and events strongly suggest U.S. Quacks and their undercover resources continually sought to disqualify and to physically harm him, [end his existence] through surreptitious acts and psychological trickery! Whereby they followed him and attempted to create justification via ruse perpetration for their activity. Ruses were geared to prove their notion of criminality that did not exist. Being absolute failures, though, because reality did not support their unsupportable hell bound efforts—by now [2013] one would think they would realize they can not create Phil's reality by inserting [primarily girly] entrapments in to his daily activities; the mindsets behind the activity are just foolish yesteryear perpetrators with "Grandiose" nonsense schemes. Being liable, they are now being called out to justify their activity or pay damages!

Yet it seems that failure to achieve the unachievable, in hindsight, did not end their ruse efforts? They decided to double down and continue their efforts with increase in vigor as if the past silliness attempts do not portray what to expect in the future? This effort appears to laymen [like Phil] to be consistent with a form of nonsense and or ridiculous American logic—certainly faulty Mental Masturbation? It is highly probable that they continue the effort because they know their target, Phil Duse, has no legal recourse to stop their activity—this suit seeks to correct the no legal recourse issue.

Or perhaps they continue their efforts believing they are so smart that reality it self is actually resident in their mindsets and conclusions i.e., where by Mental Masturbations can be pursued through the concept of "Prolepsis." Qualified to be: "the representation or assumption of a future act or development as if presently existing or accomplished." And that would eventually bring about success for their trickery concepts—no such luck reality rules.

Unfortunate for their efforts, Phil Duse is not now nor has he ever been a criminal, as in loser. He has exposed their no merit efforts over the years in his books and now has the intent to use their efforts as the basis for suit proving [at least] defamation, by the very nature of the no merit girly and entrapment activity which can be shown to be pure "Prolepsis in fact." Meaning the activity is not covered by or exempt from the constitutional laws that serve to protect U.S. law abiding citizens, violated by continual no merit prolepsis activity. Sorry Quacks, reality is not limited to the thoughts conjured by your mindsets, in spite of presumed extraordinary smartness, pureness of intent, reality is reality of its own accord—ruses, lies and deceit do not eliminate the reality of reality, it does, however, uncovers foolish behavior.

Phil wants to see if the U.S. legal systems will uphold reality or Quack claims to eliminate or suspend reality to ensure Quacks are given "God Like" assumption and or prediction authority without it being concurred on by U.S. law or law abiding U.S. citizens. It would appear that their continual ruses and entrapment scenarios are without consequence in U.S. Law? Obviously this is where we disagree, based on the activity being pure "Prolepsis"—regardless of any and all claims to the contrary.

By suit, [Phil and others who may be similarly situated] need to "first" force the legal system that authorizes or condones the activity to disclose the claimed rationale by which reasonable persons [certainly my council] will also conclude there was sufficient justification; as in reality based facts not supposition or mental masturbation beliefs of no true merit to other than Quacks and their ilk.

Yes it is understood that Quacks involved will go to every extreme of trickery to prevent the system that authorizes the activity from disclosing the results of their authorizations. Because in the absence of criminality that would too easily prove "Prolepsis" activity, at the exclusion of all other rational fact derived determinations. But, and finally, after 28 + years and a jury verdict on liability that should lead to a legal turn off button with compensation for victims of such activity, specifically Phil Duse and supporters of the suit.

SUIT ISSUES FOLLOW

SUIT ISSUE # 1: The suit will establish: Prolepsis by Quack (possibly at the behest of a fired and transferred Southern Officer for racism) inclusion of a ridiculous note/claim in medical records (from a Quack entity who never met Phil Duse whereby a claim of standing or other authorization to render such adverse conclusions (on a person with top job ratings and a top secret clearance to boot) could have a proper basis or other legal standing to claim authorization to render defamation of a subject not interviewed.

Phil needs the U.S. legal system to force uncovering of whatever the claims for reasonable persons to see what was rendered as if it was true; as opposed to being, by process of elimination, action in support of a third party (COTR) with a no merit axe to grind against Phil Duse—or possibly to support the initiator of the "out of the blue" surveillance, or the on going girly ruses and entrapment scenarios, to include initiator/

contributor to "hit men" wanting to terminate Phil's existence of this earth. The disclosures would constitute justice for Phil as well as those who may one day find themselves similarly situated.

The entities Phil worked for who provided guidance council and direction that he followed did not commission or otherwise request such harming information—but some one [perpetrator] had to have initiated such a request—leaving the culprit of choice to be a COTR or as stated above whoever initiated "out of the blue" surveillance activity, [or DCIS or other Government entity?] neither of which had grounding to render defamatory insults as if they were true.

Moreover, this perpetrator claims/states "releasing such information could harm you [meaning Phil Duse] without addressing the "open" issue of defamation which the presumed Quack author brought to the table—to game the legal system [such as falsely claiming a contractor was the culprit] to avoid obvious liability appears to be the more appropriate reality based reasoning doesn't it?

It would appear to reasonable persons that the false damming defamatory information was released to "demonize" Phil Duse for his work history and prevent future assignments of the kinds of highly technical logistical related jobs managers assigned to him? And he has had no recourse to challenge and or correct the blatantly false characterization that can't be disclosed to him because "it could harm him"—Phil agrees on the harm nature. Yes on its face it is defamation by "prolepsis" and therefore clearly actionable in a suit. Assuming Constitutional protections (4th Amendment) have meaning in law to protect U.S. law-abiding citizens against the perpetrators who boldly, in writing, commit defamation by mental masturbation conclusions?

The perpetrators/Quacks need only to prove the admitted to harming intention is justified in a court of law; not in a group of COTRs or by Quack mental masturbation determination. Whoever the offending party is they should not be able to claim protection of some sort [can share their defamations with anyone but Phil] without having authorization for the action in the beginning—-yes it did harm Phil Duse immensely [promotion and length of service leading to premature retirement] and continues to do so—28 years of harm and still counting.

SUIT ISSUE # 2: As noted in other Phil Duse books, he has been the target of individuals wanting to terminate his existence. They communicated their murderous intent by causing two "Hit Men" to appear in a vehicle parked in front of his driveway in Stafford, VA, one of which drew a hand gun and aimed it at his spouse as she approached his car to look for his check book, apparently/probably thinking it was Phil possibly because she was wearing his house coat. The obvious culprit would be whoever initiated the "out of the blue" surveillance activity implicating Phil in a non-existing act of criminality!

Fortunately, he did not fire the weapon because the second person in the vehicle recognizing it wasn't Phil hollered "don't shoot it is not him". The startled shooter repeated the comment "don't shoot"? Got back in the vehicle and they speed away with tires screeching. Phil "dumfounded observed the intent of the hit men from the doorway leading to his garage—Who caused or is otherwise responsible for this intended fatal incident—obviously as stated above the entity who initiated or otherwise caused the "out of the blue" surveillance activity is involved, which ties back to the Government in some way as only they have the resources to engage in the continuous surveillance activity experienced by Phil for over 28 years! Phil believes the FBI is involved in addition to nefarious Quacks?

SUIT ISSUE # 3: Phil's daily news paper were sprayed with a caustic chemical that reacts to touch of skin, entering ones physical body and upon reaching the heart brings about a very rapid heartbeat, in spite of no exertion by the chemical's victim. The next occasion Phil detected the chemical's unique odor on his newspaper and the rapid hart rate ensued after it touched his skin, he immediately went to the Woodbridge VA military dispensary and had blood work drawn in an attempt to identify the chemical causing the rapid heart beat.

Unfortunately, the medical facility could not determine what was causing the rapid heart increase in spite of no physical activity? Phil still has one of the offending news papers, hopefully today's technology can determine the name of the chemical that causes the noted increase in heart beating; afterwards things will really get interesting in terms of who produced it and who did they delivered the chemical spray and salve products to?

SUIT ISSUE # 4: Hit Men in Altoona, PA: on 12 October 2004, Phil was away from his residence between 2 and 3 pm to run errands. Only Phil and his spouse occupied the single-family residence, his spouse was at work, Altoona MACYs. The next day, 13 October 2004, in the morning while taking a shower he discovered a dollop [one inch] of salve had been placed on his washcloth. Phil lathered up thinking the dollop was hair cream placed there by his wife thinking she had grabbed the wrong washcloth. To his surprise, Phil discovered the salve was the caustic chemical he had previously encountered on his morning newspapers in a spray form. In that only one other person was in the house and that person could not have had knowledge of or otherwise acquired this unknown dangerous caustic chemical, a third party with the chemical in salve form entered Phil's house and caused the deposit of the chemical on his wash cloth.

Phil notes that it could not have been his spouse—who otherwise would have to have been duped in some disingenuous inauspicious way and Phil has no interest in pursuing this line of reasoning, but the perpetrator who provided the chemical certainly would and is the guilty party regardless of any other factors? If this assumption is wrong a simple polygraph will surely uncover the perpetrating culprit? Notice of this incident was provided in one of Phil's books of which a copy was provided to the U.S. Attorney General's office—no response—yet.

Unfinished and/or not yet resolved legal/suit business

As stated herein, Phil provided notice of third party surreptitious surveillance activity to the DCIS [Defense Criminal Investigating Service] in connection with their investigation on inventory losses by a contractor under Phil's property accounting responsibility—they informed Phil they would investigate the issue and he should take no further action, Phil complied. The DCIS later falsely informed Phil that the instant contractor was the culprit behind the surveillance but they were other than truthful, the instant contractor played no part whatsoever. Eventually Phil left that position to accept a higher graded position offered to him exclusively by the Navy Air System Command. While working for the Navy Air System Command, Phil discovered [two years after initial report to DCIS] two females from the DCIS office were involved in the on going sleuthing activity?

His next Government job assignment required securing a "Top Secret" clearance requiring a back ground investigation of Phil from age 5 forward. Phil accepted the job offered by this "Top Secret" contract organization; it required him to train all Property Administrators in the organization on the new Property Administration manual DOD-4160.2-M, for which he was one of the authors.

In connection with this job, Phil was formally informed he would be/is now subject to top-secret intelligence sanctions regarding his job responsibilities. For example, Phil was obligated to report, under sanction of going to jail for failure, any and all suspicious activity by third parties due to the top secret critical nature of this position and responsibilities inherent in dealing with top secret information—Phil fully understood the arena he was now working in and quickly complied with reporting requirements to inform them of the on going suspicious surveillance activity previously reported to the DCIS.

Note that the report of "out of the blue" activity by unknown persons was still an open issue. Phil reported the activity in writing to the appropriate official in his new organization; the official ensured Phil appropriate investigative action would be initiated. Phil again believed what the official stated and awaited the results—but once again he was being fooled? The no investigation result of the presumed investigation is unbelievable in its obvious intent and purpose to not engage the proper investigative activity [DCIS] who could have resolved the issue simply by telling the truth.

The official rendered the investigation request to other than the DCIS: U.S. Air Force Office of Special Investigations (AFOSI) and that activity had absolutely no jurisdiction or other authority to conduct an investigation of a person not subject to their jurisdiction let alone resolve the issues at hand. Phil reporting of the issues to appropriate authorities to include EEOC and earlier suits have not resolved the issues, there has been no justice for Phil—yet.

Therefore, Phil still seeks justice on these issues as hind sight clearly indicates the issues at hand are the undeniable bottom lines still screaming for resolution: COTR—"were going to get you"; out of the blue—life disrupting surveillance; hit-men—multiple attempts; on going girly ruses and entrapment attempts—pure no merit prolepsis: **ALL CREATED FROM ILLUSIONARY WHOLE CLOTH!** By suit Phil seeks compensation and a turn off button for himself and could apply for others who one day find themselves being subjected to this kind of **"no merit"** prolepsis activity perpetrated over decades against Phil Duse with no end in sight!

CHAPTER 6

CONTACTS FOR PURPOSE OF PROVING DEFAMATION

Before we identify contacts it would prove useful to this task to first define the ruse and entrapment arena created by intrusion of perpetrating Quacks and their ilk—the fruits of their presumed so smart devious-silliness.

In addition to their unwelcome intrusive presence in his work environments: Navy Air Systems Command, Defense Logistic Agency's Contract Management Command, Phil unlike most others in the U.S. had to endure their unrelenting sleuthing at routinely visited venues: provisioning for foods, gardening supplies, clothing, furniture, and appliances and at entertainment events with career comrades [Officer Clubs] as well as on typical family vacationing—cruise ships, coast to cost car traveling vacations to National Parks, San Francisco, Canada and Air Flight to the Bahamas—where he was routinely demonized to gain support from venue management—in spite of no criminality.

At these venues, when available, he would participate in Casino gaming and or horse race wagering. To his initial surprise, perpetrators followed and had made their presence known to the managers of the venues [apparent pre demonization requirement to engage in sleuthing] thus changing the venues from their stated ethical licensed operations to prospective Quack entrapment locations for prolepsis activity that also engaged venue security resources in supporting roles! The undeniable fact of no criminality on the part of Phil did not stay their hands—why not, how is this authorized—if not authorized, who is liable for the defamation inherent in the execution of the process?

PROLEPSIS: is it not an undeserved consequence directed at Phil mandated by Quacks? As it regards Officer Clubs, in spite of Phil being both a law-abider and Officer Club member for decades? Spending time at the above noted venues, unlike other patrons, gave third party Quack resources [primarily females but a few presumed uncle toms too] a presumed opportunity to intervene in his activities in a "you don't know but we're very slick and smart and seek to entrap you." Clearly yesteryear activity unique to American sleuthing behaviors where they operate as though they are above constitutional protections mandated in the IV Amendment. It is truly amazing how they assume by their presumed smartness that they "fit in" as if their intrusion activities and intentions coincided with, were agreeable to, or otherwise inimical to Phil's social intentions instead of the reality that they were strangers acting strangely?

If the above conclusion is correct, it is a ridiculous psychological notion on it face, particularly in Officer Clubs that Phil socialized in, [location of initial discovery] as they did not demonstrate or appear to understand normal nuisances and idiocy centric behaviors part and parcel to professional military officers at Walter Reed in DC and the Fort Belvoir, VA, Officers Clubs.

Phil and most others in the club noted they were clearly civilian fakers not accustomed to a military social environment—what were they up to and why? We could see their predicament but they didn't, possibly a shortcoming in their sleuthing training. By and large they were either given no position within the conversation group or politely ignored by the other officers, who would often leave the gathering in discus wondering what was the real deal—later it became clear to several of the officers [who informed Phil] that he was their target? Yet they always failed what ever their intent; the silly reasoning came and left with them!

Whatever their reasoning, Phil's social friends wanted no part in their sleuthing; Phil lost comrades who no longer participated in weekly gatherings-those still in the area will be contacted by Phil—apparently Quacks either see little value in Army comrades associating or stupidly associate it with civilian criminal grouping?

Whatever their sleuthing intentions they were "in fact" as stated earlier strangers acting strangely clearly noted by Phil and most others with extensive experience dealing with "American" behaviors in a non military context where a smile can be misinterpreted and often does not mean what it otherwise can be presumed to mean—it's an American civilian thing that certainly differs from Europeans and typical Asians/American social environments in Phil's experience—which is far grater than most Quacks. Some, not Phil who voted for republicans since Ronald Reagan as they are more supportive of Defense Department priorities, call it a Republican "I'm" being nice to you but only in this instance behavior. Maybe the smiling when nothing is funny gives them away?

For purposes of this suit Phil will list the venues, commercial and others, that he visited over the years for his council's consideration regarding noted sleuthing; he will revisit them as necessary to request those with knowledge on the issues in this case to come forward, and possibly participate in any liability rewards because in the final analysis they were being victimized by a hidden hand of prevaricators who unlike the innocent venues are guilty in fact, [IV amendment violations] regardless of prolepsis activity predicated on or assumes their target is guilty—or will be eventually.

The venue's employees are guilty of nothing, as assisting liars is not a automatic crime when the liars fool you to get your support—so the issue at hand is—prevaricating is prevaricating regardless of claims to the contrary claiming some form of justification—such as we are Quacks authorized to lie in connection with sleuthing and perpetrator activities. Who else says that [amongst innocents] and where is it stated and or authorized by codification in U.S. law?

Then or now the issue becomes the legal concept of one being presumed innocent unless proven guilty in a court of law. Prolepsis activity invalidates and turns that concept on its head, as the target is demonized as guilty and the reasoning becomes a Quack preference, which instills that concept to replace the reality of who you are in fact. Your reality should be the reality and not an unprovable mental masturbation concept!

It is highly probable that Quacks will be more or less forced to revisit the venues to instruct them not to divulge previous sleuthing agreements—maybe they will maybe they won't but that is yet to be conclusively decided! It is undecided? Yes because Quacks incorrectly appear to believe they are above or beyond the laws at issue! Meaning in retrospect that each innocent previously fooled can now become a contributor to the suit when they come forward; and will represent another nail and or foot in the perpetrators posteriors. That is unless the perpetrators are to slick for reality in spite of their silliness?

The venues and individuals mentioned in Phil's book are but a good starting place to mine [as in a rich source of supply] individuals with first hand knowledge on Quack prolepsis activity. The story line of the books are non fictional and provide specific details on who what when and why from the perspective of a long suffering victim—Phil Duse.

SIDE BARS

A: FUNDING THE SUIT?

Phil is committed to providing the first $5,000 dollars towards funding the suit and the proceeds from sales of this book will go into the kitty also. It is understood that it is highly unlikely a lawyer/law firm will undertake processing the suit on a contingency basis—but hope springs internal and the lawyer/law firm, if not on a contingency basis, can secure agreement from Phil for up to 33% of any eventual award [suit will request and is worth millions] with the remaining portion divided 50% to contributing supporters and 50% to Phil Duse.

The ultimate winners, however, will be the law abiding people of the U.S.—and the IV Amendment to enforce the notion that what's right is right—then we the people and not nefarious Quacks and their ilk will relegate prolepsis activity to a proper second or lower place in comparison with "innocent until proven guilty" in a court of law.

Thus eliminating prolepsis assignment of guilt to disrupt law-abiders lives without consequence or through mental masturbation conclusion of no merit or "Cat Birders" trickery. We can do this but we/you must stand up to be counted as belonging to "Today's Law-Abiders of the U.S. If you recognize the merit and value inherent in a suit to ensure your IV Amendment rights are upheld, contribute what you can to the suit's processing! Monies not spent on the suit will be returned to the sender—a Phil Duse promise.

Send funding contribution to:
Phil Duse, 130 Frederick Road, Altoona, PA 16602
Contact information:
Fax: 814-944-3846
Email: philduse@atlanticbb.net
Cell phone: 814-931-6388 (for prospective council)

While the suit is being processed it is also understood that the defendants (Quacks and their ilk) will undertake every opportunity to finish their ongoing "Kill the Messenger" job. Their ruses will continue unabated because the perpetrators have all necessary resources, financial and personnel, to waste in attempts to obfuscate the issues as well as continue girly and entrapment ruses. Their ultimate goal can "only" be to bring about an ending similar to what happens in about 90% of complaints processed by the EEOC—Heads they win Tails you lose. But and regardless of their chicanery this suit effort will continue until Phil leaves the scene. Yet he reminds you of the time tested notion "If you don't stand up for something you'll sit down for any thing." Phil will continue to stand up for what's right into perpetuity—that's a promise and not a dream.

B: QUACK TURN OFF BUTTON

The nature of the issues in this case require a "Court Ordered" turn off button as it is the operation of the courts that in someway through Quack "gaming" the system that authorized and or condoned the no merit prolepsis activities against this proud law abiding citizen name Phillip M. Duse. Why they undertook this multi decade effort is a mystery unknown to Phil Duse except as noted herein regarding third parties identified in this book. What is known: Phil Duse has constitutional rights that were not only trampled on but almost resulted in his death—then no one but the instigating "Quacks" would have known why—that in and of itself is unacceptable to all Americans!

Their more outlandish 2013 ruses: nonsense interfaces by strangers acting strangely at the Rocky Gap Casino Resort in Maryland and during his vacationing in the Bahamas, demonstrate the Quack perpetrators have no intention of ending their no merit prolepsis activity. Their emphasis' appears to be the silly continuation of ruses exercised by "strangers, acting strangely" as if strangers by some form or fashion could justify the nonsense activity. Phil does not fellowship with stranger's period. Phil's response remains the same—ignore all idiotic behaviors portrayed by whomever—the instigators just don't know any better—poor things. His message to Quack mind sets directing the activity is captured in the comment "KMA" the first word of the acronym is kiss.

C: THE EEOC "THE REAL DEAL"

Unrelated to the issues in this suit but of interest to the thousands fooled, like Phil, into believing the EEO/EEOC is an appropriate forum for aggrieved persons, harmed through no fault of their own, to receive justice is: replace the EEOC with an entity separate in every way from the current non independent management structure. The book entitled "EEOC The Real Deal" suggests Quacks and lawyers engineered an injustice process so fraught with loopholes that the process itself is actually the problem.

What's stated next qualifies as a "Rosetta Stone" type example on what is promised versus the reality of what is "falsely" delivered with immunity. Readers should refer to the book "EEOC The Real Deal" ISBN 1-410-4654-1 for a more detailed account that specifically highlights how a complaint to the EEO/EEOC, traveled through lower courts to end at the door step of the Supreme Court was purposely "grossly" miss interpreted at every stop to render the complaint to be not viewed through unbelievable trickery in the process, in spite of the inherent injustice communicated in the complaint.

EEOC PROMISE UNDER PROHIBITED EMPLOYMENT PRACTICES: The laws forbid discrimination in every aspect of employment! Don't believe it as truth will be absent.

The scenario that ignored the presumed law:

Phil obtained a Top Secret Clearance and was hired for a 'Top Secret" position with prosecutable restrictions for divulging information to any person or entity not cleared to receive the information, meaning not in possession of a Top Secret Clearance.

Yet a person who was not his supervisor of record, as proven by the fact he had no knowledge of his job responsibilities, [because he did not have the requisite clearance to question let alone to receive the job information] testified, shooting from the hip, acting as if he had actual knowledge of Phil's position—see page 262—and authority to rate Phil's work that he had absolutely no knowledge of—resulting in a testimony of bald faced lies! Also called "Agency Articulations" that are both unproven and unprovable, but inimical of justice denied regardless of facts!

The EEOC accepted the testimony, in spite of objections, as if it was valid yet the testimony was impossible on its face not just improper. The undeniable conclusion: this EEOC routine acceptance of false testimony renders the process to be a that of a "Kangaroo Court" a sham similar in nature to an Indian Treaty of yore—the truth can be ignored or otherwise has no place in the process just because there is no penalty for defendant lies?

In that defendants can routinely call their articulations proper regardless of facts to the contrary means they will routinely win; as they have for decades. The reality of the process difference [between EEOC adjudications and this book] is: Phil agrees to take a polygraph on any and all comments made by him in this book, in a let the chips fall where they may manner!

The people can create a better more just process: assuming the EEOC process is changed to permit aggrieved complainants to take a polygraph in support of their testimony—this scenario would produce a difference in findings that would invalidate essentially all rendering based on untruthful "Agency Articulations" as occurred in Phil's case. Thus expose automatic acceptance of defendants lies, in spite of facts to the contrary, to be the reason why defendants win 90% of cases. The current process has been engineered to permit defendants to easily excise/eliminate truths to manage who will receive justice—based on other than truth in testimony or fact based findings!

Therefore as the above side bar relates to this suit, the Phil Duse reality is and has, more importantly, always been: he does not fellow ship with liars of any stripe; let alone perpetrator resources attempting to interface as if they are other than the strangers acting strangely which is what they are in fact—regardless of psychological intent of Quacks, the interface can't pass the basic smell test to not be ignored.

Quack presumed smartness in causing the attempted interfaces does not change the no merit reality it just suggest gross stupidity on their part or a lack of relevant training!

ENCLOSURES

First Page of:

Comment by R. Galgon Cpt MC disclosing information surreptitiously entered in records

Letter to M&T Bank regarding suspect non professional behaviors of Manager

Letter to Logan Valley Mall Management regarding insulting comments by Mall Cops

Freedom of Information Act/Privacy request regarding Air Force Special Investigation

Letters reporting improper activity to Managers of:

Altoona Regional Health System—1

Altoona VA Hospital—3

Holiday Inn and Choice Hotels—1 ea

Letters to News Media—3

Letter referring issues to US Supreme Court—2

Other Phil Duse Books: *False Color of Authority* and *EEOC: The Real Deal*

Phillip M. Duse

TO: Treasurer's Office
      6900 Georgia Ave., NW
      Hosp Treasurer's Off
      Washington DC 20307-5001

August 7, 2003

From: Duse, Phillip M. (195-32-5846)
       55 Spring Lake Dr
       Stafford VA 22556 (previously 22554)

RE: Hospital Invoice and Receipt (Inpatient charges for period stated below)
      Period: 24 Jul thru 27 Jul and 28 Jul thru 31 Jul 03

Dear Sir or Madam,

Enclosed herewith is check #8653 for $48.60, inpatient charges at $8.10 per day for a total of 6 days.

New issue: I noted a comment on the WR Narrative Sum & Pt D/C (30 Jul 2003) entered by Richard Galgon Cpt MC 6481, with reference to " WR Psych History & Physical and WR Psych Resident Admit Note." This "note" has not been clarified to this inpatient as to its meaning and intent or other reasoning regarding why it exist in my records. I am curious as to who caused such information to be placed in my file and under what authority. I am also curious as to how one can challenge the propriety of such authority, in that it appears to be a surreptitious comment?

As a pass litigant of actions alleged against Governmental entities, the subject of two books,"Phil Duse Versus the Tyranny of DOD and EEOC: The Real Deal" I respectfully request the information under this note be provided; for my review and edification in order to gage its appropriateness.

I have a natural concern that such undefined information may contain hidden meanings that, among other possibilities, would be of curiosity interest to my readers. Further, it may prove to expose additional underhanded activities of Government not generally or widely written about, as it relates to minority complaintants in general and specifically to this minority. It could in its self prove to be of valuable research and editorial interest on "real life truths" that should be shared with laymen interested in how Government actions could serve to support third party interest! Retaliation is the possible operative issue, but who knows no explanation was provided!

Your response or lack thereof may be shared with my readers.

Phillip M. Duse

Phil Duse Exposes: Government Quack Silliness

Phillip M. Duse

130 Frederick RD, Altoona PA 16602

March 6, 2013

M&T Bank
Attn: Management
P.O. Box 767
Buffalo, NY 14240-0767

Dear Sir or Madam

RE: Interface regarding local Bank's apparent support of long standing efforts initiated, allegedly, by Government Quacks/Dolts to maximize unique disingenuous "race bating" entrapments to harm the undersigned. Probably in retaliation for long past events regarding forced reimburse for inappropriate charges to government contracts under my audit control. It is unfortunate that the inappropriate suspect behavior is no longer limited to Quacks and their ilk as it now appears to include your manager in the Pleasant Valley Office. In previous encounters he gave only typical professional responses; our last meeting brought forth the shocking exception shared below. Be advised that my extensive race relation training, interface experiences as a contract auditor and sense on personal integrity do not permit me to respond unprofessionally or otherwise engage retaliatory behaviors in spite of provocation. Such behavior, when handled professionally, is reportable to an upper managerial level, and one need not respond in kind or otherwise consider exhibiting similar unprofessional behaviors: except when quacks, dolts or klan types are the driving force, then a civil suit may be the best solution.

1. Consider: On 2 March I, Phillip M. Duse, visited the above office to transact typical first of month banking business, through interface with the office manager. After completing the transactions, I turned to exit the office and, unexpectedly in my peripheral vision, noticed he appeared to express dissatisfaction with my presence; through antics equivalent to a "ghetto" middle finger salute. I gave no response and departed the bank, typical to how I respond to such racially tinged or otherwise inappropriate situations. Given this was the first response of this nature from this manager, it smelled like a Quack initiative or possibly an act from one fighting personal demons, called LDP's in my books- [little d___k people]. There was no precursor event on my part.

2. Also consider: When I moved from Virginia to Altoona in 2004, I changed my bank accounts from a Virginia bank managing my accounts for 24 years, with absolutely no unprofessional issues, to a local Altoona banker. This banker informed that my Altoona arrival brought a swarm of Government investigators. The initial professional interface began to deteriorate. I changed banks to your bank, to avoid unprofessional behaviors. I suspect the deteriorations are the result of or otherwise based on long standing no merit Quack based demonization of my personhood. These entities, for the last 25-30 years, have engaged in demonization activity: girly ruses to support un-sundry entrapment scenarios, occurring coast to coast to include the Bahamas (2013) and cruse vacation (2003) as well as in hotels, Casinos and medical offices. I have written several books on the subject; the Quacks appear to consider themselves to be above/beyond the law and will remain so [given the decades] until their mental masturbations are exhausted and reality comes to the fore through a defamation suit.

3. To address this issue, I will attempt to do my future banking in your facility located on 17th street; otherwise I will attempt to capture future similar evens, if they occur, as they unfold on tape or camcorder. If that fails I will, unfortunately, be forced to change banks again to avoid being drawn into silly unprofessional confrontational events.

Phillip M. Duse

Logan Valley Mall
Attention Management
5580 Good-lane Road
Altoona, PA 16602

May 18, 2011

RE: Insulting comments from Mall (Police) Officer/Official

Background: On 17 May 2011, the wife and I had cause to visit your Mall's "Lens Crafter" store: my wife initiated actions to complete the purchase of a pair of new glasses. There being no customer waiting area in Lens Crafter, I sat on the bench outside the store. After five minutes or so, a uniform Mall Officer approached to my front and from 10-15 feet away, initiated in an alarming aggressive manner considering he is a complete stranger to me an inappropriate disparaging comment including the terms "bud or buddy" as if addressing a kid in a scolding manner.

I note here that such comments is an in appropriate form of address to a complete stranger—I am not his bud or buddy and had absolutely no reason to interface with him on any issue or level.

A few minutes latter another individual approached and loudly repeated the bud/buddy in a more aggressive manner yet! His comments were certainly not consistent with his bud/buddy exhortation to suggest he had some prior interface with me--alarming the vendor in the nearby pretzel stand in addition to the undersigned. The actions clearly suggested existence of a problem, to all within range of his voice, regarding my presence out side of Lens Crafter necessitating his comments. I note here that I had no ideas who this individual was or his reasoning for his inappropriate comments to a stranger shopping in the Logan Valley Shopping Mall.

I reentered Lens Crafter and mentioned the unnerving events to the sales person conversing with my wife. She identified the second person as "a creepy guy with a white beard/hair" indicating he is employed in some capacity at your Mall.

Request: whatever drove the actions of your employees is not consistent with responsible behavior to a Mall shopper—in absence of any inappropriate behaviors on his part—and your employees should be advised not to repeat the behavior. My sense of professionalism does not permit me to respond in kind, my preference is to inform management of the activity and seek legal redress if it occurs on future visits.

But, it is your Mall so please inform: If I should not shop in your mall or appear in response to solicitations such as the enclosed emails from Mall vendors. If there is some third party driving the behaviors—highly likely? Please advise me of your position in response to this letter, if you care to give one, so I can seek redress in an appropriate legal

Phil Duse Exposes: Government Quack Silliness

DEFENSE LOGISTICS AGENCY
HEADQUARTERS
8725 JOHN J. KINGMAN ROAD, SUITE 2533
FT. BELVOIR, VIRGINIA 22060-6221

APR 2 4 1996

IN REPLY
REFER TO   CAAS

Mr. Phillip M. Duse
55 Spring Lake Drive
Stafford, VA 22554

Dear Mr. Duse:

This is in reply to your Freedom of Information Act/Privacy Act request referred to us by the Air Force of Special Investigations (AFOSI) by letter dated March 20, 1996.

Review of our files did not disclose any information identifiable with you. However, AFOSI provided us a copy of our May 28, 1992 letter to them requesting their assistance in responding to complaints you made. The letter and your memo for record, dated April 6, 1992, to which our letter pertains, are enclosed.

I trust this satisfies your request.

Sincerely,

MILES R. LEHMANN
Colonel, USA
Staff Director
Command Security Office

Enclosures

Phillip M. Duse

Phillip M. Duse Sr.

130 Frederick Rd. Altoona PA 16602

September 5, 2013

Altoona Regional Health System
Altoona Hospital Campus
620 Howard Avenue
Altoona, PA 16601-4899
    Attn: Legal Department

Dear Sir or Madam:

The intent of this letter is two fold: (1) bring to your attention highly suspect, apparent, unprofessional events from a unique perspective based on years of experience with similar events; (2) The events appear to render your health care claim to be an oxymoronic term actually meaning health care and ruse host. It is on this basis compelling, as the apparent victim/target of the activity, to memorialize examples apparently clearly attributable to parties employed by or otherwise associated with your hospital. Activity in all probability driven by protagonist utilizing the very TRICARE Health care system necessitating use of your facility—something alleged for the first time here but not yet proven.

Some of the events "alleged" detailed in the new book "False Color of Authority" [Publisher Xlibris Book ID 36809], and this communication provided to TRICARE authorities for explanation—if they care to give one. By this letter, request you initiate corrective actions to forego future reoccurrence, to the extent it may have existed it is not representative of healthcare.

Unfortunately, I can not with the requisite degree of legal certainty identify a "specific" responsible person as "the" contriver or instigator but the obvious probable catalyst, as identified in the above named book of details alleging false color activities assigns the US Government to be the perpetrator. Activities now readily provable by the new technology called Brain fingerprinting: "functional magnetic resonance imaging [fmri]—technology that could thwart unwitting participants from engaging in no merit entrapments against a targeted patron.

Assuming the US Government is the catalyst; know that they are emperors without clothes seeking to "create" an offense utilizing obliging entities such as your hospital while hiding their involvement. They continue to engage in blatant defamation against this law-abiding party, but they aren't held for damages. The technology is here, meaning their defamation activity is now provable by disinterested sponsor of the fmri test! A disinterested party such as your hospital can remove itself from all possible liability by sponsoring the testing, any guilty party, of course, will oppose the testing; the undersigned agrees to fully participate in a let-the-chips-fall where they may manner, it is the most viable solution to assuage the events alleged to let the truth be known!

Qualifying Events

       On 10 November 2004 [my birthday] I drove my wife to your sister hospital located in Latrobe, PA, for a medical procedure. On or about 12 noon, went to the cafeteria and sat at the counter to order lunch. There was a young female employee behind the counter and two other female patrons sitting at the counter areas. The phone rang and the female employee informed the caller "yes he's here sitting at the counter", she hung up and continued whatever she had been doing. A couple minutes passed and the phone rang again, this time she said in a frustrated manner "okay, okay". She hung up the phone and walked directly from behind the counter to where [only] I sat and stood next to me exhibiting what I viewed as a silly grin—appearing to await some sexist action on my part.

Suspecting some kind of entrapment was in the making, as her actions were inimical of the hordes of ruses continually initiated by presumed government entities over a 20–year or so period. I immediately left the counter area and returned to the waiting area outside of my wife's treatment area, concerned that once again I was targeted for a girly ruse entrapment of some sort–but like all others to no avail.

For certain: such apparent defamation entrapment type activity is not consistent with the goals of the TRICARE program, therefore the ultimate perpetrators [US Government] were acting under a false color of authority utilizing your employees to assist in staging of their ruse against an innocent, again now easily provable by fmri testing. That was just one of several similar events occurring in the last two years, others are detailed in the above referenced book and include:

Events occurring on or about 28 July 06 in your Altoona facility in the ER area, and the waiting area outside the ER and also at the local Altoona Pizza hut on route 220 immediately after the wife and I departed the Altoona facility—staging of another girly related ruse under similar scenarios.

Administrative Events?

Altoona Regional Health System, Patient Financial Services letter dated 09/23/06, regarding service date 07/28/06, Enclosure one: The letter dated 9-23-06 and speaks to delinquency in payment by primary insurance provider–they were not delinquent. The letter appears to be premature by five days before expiration of time for the insurance provider to make payment. Is this a form of harassment! The insurance provider made payment within the allotted 30-day time-period or not later than 10/23/06. No correcting letter or letter of apology sent just notice to the "guarantor" of his responsibility when the Altoona Patient Financial Services office was at fault.

Then to add insult to injury, the patient, Cynthia A. Duse, receives two separate billings identified by separate numbers: SB: 8000 and SB: 21057–$30.00 each. We sent a payment check for each billing. A check came back falsely annotated "Paid bill twice". No mention made as to why two billings sent initially? Just another administrative problem; fault assigned to this patron?

Sincerely,

Phillip M. Duse

Patron/victim of weird hospital care
Cc TRICARE Health System

Phillip M. Duse

Phillip M. Duse

120 Frederick Road, Altoona PA 16602/944-3845/fax: 944-3846

September 5, 2013

James E. Van Zandt VAMC
2907 Pleasant Valley Boulevard
Altoona, PA 16602-4377

RE: Your Letter 503/00 dated Jun 11, 2008 and my previous letters dated Apr 2 & Apr 30 (Encl 1 & 2)

Dear Sir or Madam:

Concerns: (1) Be advised that your letter dated Jun 11, 2008 appears to miss characterize comments and intent of the previous letters at issue; therefore, I refer you to enclosures one and two, copies of the original letters, to note they do not state as you suggest "you requested to have all primary care appointments cancelled until this pharmacy issue is resolved."

(2) It is somewhat confusing as your letter goes to issues such as medications available or not under Tricare which is already known and stated, as if the comment represents new information?

(3) There is no issue regarding care/medications predicated on "future appointments" the issue is medications and care such as the prescription quoted and podiatry appointment previously approved then summarily withdrawn yet without factual explanation in any of your responses. For whatever reasons, your comments appear to refer to concerns communicated as if they are contested future care issues or could otherwise be qualified as applicable to "future care/appointments" that now must be re-authorized when there was/is no "future request"?

(4) I note that I can not force VA compliance with, for example, previously written prescriptions or podiatry appointments, which are issues that drove the questions regarding what care am I entitled to or why care authorized previously have now been construed to become issues? Appears to suggest the reasoning is driven by VA disagreement with actions reported by the undersigned, resulting from improper "protocol" of a Pharmacy person, now being presented as if to show the victim as the ultimate party at fault based on non existing "future" appointments for care!

(5) The comment you have not addressed in my letter regarding VA support of un sundry "girly" ruse activities is documented in several books I have authored suggesting the ruse ultimate initiators to be "Government Quacks and local Dolts" and states they are perpetrators "gaming" the system. Yes, I believe "gaming" with undo VA assistance; I stand by that characterization and expect to again go to the legal mat when resources permit.

Finally, I do agree the VA has provided "quality care and services" but with the caveat "except when lending support to Quacks and Dolts," the quality and care was greatly diminished and fraught with unnecessary "drama" without explanation, representative of my experiences with the Altoona VA.

Sincerely,

Phillip M. Duse
US Army Retired, CW 2 (Two Enclosures)

Phil Duse Exposes: Government Quack Silliness

130 Frederick Road, Altoona PA 16602
Phone: 814-944-3845 Fax: 814-944-3846

Phillip M. Duse

September 5, 2013

James E. Van Zandt VAMC
2907 Pleasant Valley Boulevard
Altoona, PA 16602-4377

RE: Need clarification of confusion regarding medical care you will provide versus care entitled, in view of Red Team Nurse apparent telephonic cancellation of pharmacy care and podiatry care in contravention of VA policy—is this merely a continuation of the on-going ruses I reported?

Dear Sir or Madam:

Background: I received a letter stating appointments scheduled with Red Team and Podiatrist for 15 April 2008, letter's instructions require contacting Red Team if you cannot keep a scheduled appointment for any reason.

I contacted Red Team and asked if they (VA/Pharmacy) intend to respond to my written complaint dated January 30, 2008 reporting improper protocol (insults) of your pharmacy technician [copy enclosed] and if not—as appears to be the case--considering the long history of apparent VA supported un sundry ruse activity, I would no longer accept Red Team appointments. That is until there is a response to the 30 Jan 08 letter. If management fails to correct protocol expectations of the violating VA employee, there is a high probability the activity complained about would be repeated rendering the activity in the final analysis to be just another no merit ruse.

The Red Team Nurse then stated I would not be able to receive pharmaceutical supplies from the VA if I do not keep the 15 April Red Team appointment; she ignored or disregarded the issue of concern to me—is this appropriate? I don't think so, thus this letter to memorialize the issue for later publication or comment for professional based corrective action.

I called the Podiatrist number to see, in view of the Red Team nurse comment, if I should keep the 15 April appointment, but I have yet to receive a response. I note, however, that the Podiatrist and his staff have not engaged in the ruses given apparent support by the Red Team Doctor (certainly not most of the nurses I interfaced with) i.e., girly entrapment schemes in the VA building, parking lot, and sister hospital facilities (complaints attached) and with respect to the VA pharmacy, staff person initiation of no merit-one-sided arguments—clear indication of a ruse in process to justify involvement of a third party, (VA Police!) but the bottom line is behavior not supported by proper protocol regardless of probable ruse intent.

What are the proper rules: VA welcome information provided the undersigned in Jul of 2004 state:
(1) "Our goal is to provide quality service in a caring atmosphere. Our clinical and administrative staff strive daily to provide treatment that is courteous, compassionate, and responsive to individual needs". Certainly not my experience as compared with the unsavory instances reported in this letter—yes the VA in all other respects provided excellent service.

(2) You are currently enrolled in Priority Group 2.

Phillip M. Duse

Phillip M. Duse

130 Frederick Road, Altoona PA 16602 944-3845

September 5, 2013

James E. VanZandt Veterans Affairs Medical Center
2907 Pleasant Valley Boulevard
Attention: Manager of Pharmacy Services

Dear Sir or Madam:

The purpose of this letter is to bring to your attention the distasteful experience suffered when dealing with your pharmacy refill person on 29 January 2008 at or about 12: noon.

I had cause to go to your refill pharmacy because pills provided under prescription # 4142422 (200 two 100 pill prescriptions) were based on consumption at 3 per day rate when the actual consumption rate was 6 per day. I expressed this concern to the refill person and she, referred to her computer data base and loudly retorts for all in and outside the refill office:

"That's not right! You still have plenty of pills left"! Question: in view of the math what is this contention based on? Is it something mandated by your office/hospital specific to only Phil Duse? It appears unsupportable regardless of her premature "that's not right claim".

I suggested she should do the math, based on my consuming 42 pills a week and compare that volume with the number of pills provided (380) in three prescriptions since Aug 10,07) obviously the pills provided was insufficient, and that's why I was there! Certainly not to suffer inappropriate insults of any sort let alone a false claim of untruthfulness.

She again loudly stated to her audience,

"That's not right" as if I was still other than truthful--because my math was incorrect--and grabbed her calculator as if she could prove her insulting outbursts correct and justified. Of course she couldn't but offered no apology—she achieved her insult goal?

At this point, being totally embarrassed and insulted by this scolding behavior on her part where she communicated in a loud tone as if she was talking to an unruly teenager or worst and wanted all within range of her voice to hear the scolding she was issuing.

She then with apparent great reluctance concluded "I'll give you enough to last until the next refill is issued. Something she should have said or done at the beginning and not created clear reasoning for this complaint—unless, possibly, she was mandated to do so there are other examples.

The issue: I am due and demand a formal apology! This issue will be included with the other questionable issues reported for your edification and corrective action as you deem appropriate.

Hopefully, you will recognize this report is the only appropriate response acceptable to or forthcoming from this veteran, other than not seeking the VA medical care that I am presumably entitled to—am I being forced to pursue other care? If so, please advise as fortunately I have the option of tri-care and Medicare and the tri care mail order pharmacy. But, I memorialize this unsavory pharmacy event in this letter and will make reference to it and your response in other-future venues.

Phil Duse Exposes: Government Quack Silliness

Phillip M. Duse

130 Frederick Road, Altoona PA 16602
814-944-3845/ FAX: 814-944-3845
email: philduse@atlanticbb.net

September 5, 2013

Choice Hotels Senior Manager [Please provide this letter to Choice Hotel and other hotels]
c/o Comfort Suites
2110 North Franklin Drive
Washington, PA 15301

Dear Sir or Madam:

The purpose of this letter is twofold:

(1) Formal Complaint in protest of surreptitious intrusion activity, room #304, by US Governmental entities that was confirmed by the desk person Ms Barton, (who voiced firm disagreement with the activity) but, apparently, could not prevent it—obvious defamation of their target! The activity occurred on 07/04/08 at your Washington PA facility while I was visiting the local Casino/Racetrack. The intruding party/individual searched luggage left in the room and repositioned shirts in the luggage to where awareness of the intrusion was obvious—no maid was involved. They have engaged in this kind of activity at virtually every hotel I stayed in (10 or more stays in hotels throughout the US since my change of residence from Stafford, VA to Altoona PA in 2004,) the activity in this regard is identified in books I authored published by Xlibris: "(2004: Phil Duse Versus the Tyranny of DOD/DOJ) and 2006, "False Color of Authority" The unwary but accommodating hotel are victims of a no merit Governmental process as much as I am a victim of the burglary and defamation employed.

(2) The Government entities are and have been operation under a false color of authority to "Game" the system at the expense of gullible hotels such as your Comfort Suites who are falsely led to believe the activity is based on proper legal authority, it is not but has been hard to challenge. Now you/we can expose the culprits to be burglars "Gestapo like agents" engaging in wholesale chicanery and defamation, through the new technology of "Brain Fingerprinting", let the chips fall where they may.

As a disinterested party like multiple similarly situated hotels that has guess victimized by the activity, you need only to take the lead to challenge the perpetrators [inform hotels in general] to prove there is merit to their activity! I agree to come to whatever location to participate in the "Brain Fingerprinting test" to conclusively disprove "whatever" the claim as justification for their activity and thereby expose it to be instances of Government dolts and quacks "Gaming" the system because they are not challenged—yes I agree to share in paying the cost for the test. Who conducts such tests? The "CEPHOS Corporation, 38 Lawrence Pepperell, MA 01463 and No Lie MRI Inc., 354 Gravilla Street, LA Jolla CA 92037", please advise if you will take the lead to bring out the truths to end such activity.

Sincerely,

Phillip M. Duse Sr.
Victim of Government Defamatory Burglars

Phillip M. Duse

Phillip M. Duse Sr.

130 Frederick Road, Altoona, PA 16602

September 5, 2013

Holiday Inn Express
681 Flowing Springs Road
Ranson, WV 25438

Dear Sir or Madam:

I stayed at your hotel recently, 9/18/07 to 9/19/07, and the professional attributes of your employees and the comforts afforded by the facility were representative of the very best in hotel accommodations, I will return. But there is an issue that I feel compelled to memorialize in order to ensure you are aware of concerns and possible implications regarding criminal activity under false color.

On the 19th, morning while brushing my teeth, I discovered someone had removed almost half of the toothpaste from my new tube and attempted to distribute the remaining paste to conform to the tube's shape before the surreptitious removal. You are not at fault but have been victimized as I have.

Here's my concern: It would appear very likely individuals operating under a false color of authority (I refer to them as Government perpetrators) had entered the room for reasons of their own design? The overriding issue from my perspective is "if they removed property [tooth paste] they could also plant property of their choosing? I have written books detailing the issues references enclosed and informed other hotels where I stayed of my concern when the perpetrator activity was detected. Yes it is my intent to go to the mat of litigation at the first opportunity—knowing requisite proof is hard to come by it is a daunting challenge.

In future stays I request you inform the perpetrators of my strong disagreement with their activity as it is alleged and easily provable to be under false color of authority. You have my agreement, without other qualification, to undergo whatever truth testing procedure you or any other competent disinterested party may recommend, to disprove whatever system gaming claims they table as justification. Then the reality that they are indeed "gaming" the system using your and similarity situated hotels undue assistance. They, of course will decline the offer—thus their false color activity would be confirmable and guilty parties could be held accountable in subsequent litigation.

Nevertheless, a possible solution for your hotel in and of its self suggests your challenge for the perpetrators to table their justification claim(s) for testing of both parties by the latest technology "Functional Magnetic Resonance Imaging [fmri]" would end the false color activity. Such challenge would at least enhance the term "liar, liar" to apply to either the undersigned or to the perpetrators exposing false color of authority activity as alleged in this communication. You might mention "I have their "buddy" swinging" the term perpetrators proffered in their most recent perpetrator activity.

Sincerely,

Phillip M. Duse Sr.
Author and Government victim:
Two enc.

Phil Duse Exposes: Government Quack Silliness

Phillip M. Duse
Concerned Law Abiding Citizen

130 Frederick Road
Altoona PA 16602
814-944-3845 Fax: 814-944-3846
phillipduse@verizon.com

September 5, 2013

SUBJECT: Relevance and Reliability Testing for use of "Brain Fingerprinting Technology"

TO: Story Line Producers

48 Hours:

60 Minutes:

Dateline:

Talk Show Hosts:

Dear Sir or Madam:

We are now at a juncture in America's legal jurisprudence were anyone of your organizations can initiate the certification test on "Relevance and Reliability of Brain Finger Printing Technology." If you elect to do so, you will foster a monumental change, indeed stupendous in scope similar to DNA analysis, and forever impact, retard or inhibit obfuscations inherent in today's to often false and wholly inaccurate legal determinations. Certification of the reliability of the technology would revolutionize the ability of "people" to derive or discern undeniable truth from any respondent's reliance on tweak-able responses conjured by intellect. When they claim "I don't know or didn't do it their brain could say otherwise" people could discern undeniable truth and let the chips-fall-where-they-may.

I am available to participate in the test and have communicated testable issues, identified in two nonfiction books, all the way to the U.S. Supreme Court by writ of certiorari. I believe it is nigh time to expose the falsehoods and Government perfidy in these kinds of issues; I'll wager the Government will go to any length necessary to prevent certification, to negate their exposure and possible liability. The unanswered question at this juncture: why will they oppose testing that benefits the real truth?

Can you put the certification issues under the public's microscope on your program? To see, for example, to what degree our Government has involvement with "Hit Men" or mental masturbation pursuits under false color or authority, or openly engages in profiling/stereotyping of innocents. I suggest these kinds of issues are grounded in and part and parcel to the current system primarily because there has been no certification of the reliability of Brain Fingerprinting technology, to determine its limitation and practical applications. Can we talk about this as a story line on your program?

Sincerely,

Phillip M. Duse
Author: 2004 Phil Duse Versus the Tyranny of DOD/DOJ
And, EEOC: The Real Deal.

Phillip M. Duse

TO: CBS and (DATELINE)
524 WEST 57 STREET
New York, New York 10019-2985

December 9, 2011

From: Phillip M. Duse
130 Frederick Road
Altoona, PA 16602

RE: Idea provided in Sep. 2004 and Sep. 2006 regarding false color activities of Government; highly probable wide interest to law abiding US citizens

In the earlier communications to CBS, Dateline and other investigating news entities 20/20 etc.,. I provided detailed exerts from the then recently published books "EEOC, The Real Deal and False Color of Authority." The information exposed unsavory actions of Government entities [termed Dolts/Perpetrators] against a law abiding citizen.

The Sep. 04 response from DATELINE stated "**The idea has been noted, however, and it may inform or inspire a future DATELINE segment."**

Hence this letter to inform the news media that the information is as valid today as it was then. There is another book of interest to the issues "US Government Quacks and Dolts" that provides more information yet on the explosive issues. A copy of the manuscript was provided to the US Attorney General's office for their edification. There has been no response from the AJ office to me but the unsavory actions reported continued unabated.

Be advised that the author is still interested in presenting the issues to the US public, in a let the chips fall where they may manner. Assuming enough time has passed to inspire a future segment? Can we now talk?

Sincerely,

Phillip M. Duse Sr. 814-944-3845. philduse@atlanticbb.net

Phillip M. Duse

Concerned Law Abiding Citizen (Victim of Ruses) initiated by Government

130 Frederick Road
Altoona, PA 16602
814-944-3845, Fax 814-944-3846
phillip.duse@verizon.net

May 17, 2006

RE: Previous communications regarding conduct of test utilizing Brain Fingerprinting Technology, (Functional magnetic resonance imaging, fmri)

TO: Story Line Producers: 48 Hours; 60 Minutes; Dateline, and talk show host.

Dear Sir or Madam:

In pursuing the above RE objective: I have provided the issues, first four chapters of new book, to two commercial entities who conduct fmri [Brain Fingerprinting test]. I volunteered to the entities to undergo the test on the issues provided in a let the chips fall where they may manor—to uncover Government villains and to introduce DNA-like mechanism to protect innocent law abiding Americans.

The entities: No Lie MRI Inc. 354 Gravilla Street, LA Jolla CA 92037, Attention: Joel.

And: CEPHOS Corporation, 38 Lawrence, Pepperell, MA 01463, Attention: President.

Enclosed here with is a copy of the fourth chapter detailing what the bottom line of the issues are about, for your edification, hopping there is sufficient interest for your story line editor to take the lead to sponsor the testing. Assuming there is sufficient interest, I agree up front to participate fully in the testing as you may dictate.

I/we need a disinterested party to sponsor the test. Perhaps a Consumer Protection Agency may show interest but either of you could serve as a disinterested sponsor to bring about a monumental improvement for law abiders and American jurisprudence—all American have an interest in the outcome.

Sincerely,

Phillip M. Duse

Concerned Law Abiding Citizen

Author, Military and Government Retiree

In The
Supreme Court of the United States

----------^----------

Phillip M. Duse,
Petitioner,

v.

WILLIAM S. COHEN
Secretary of Defense,

JANET RENO,
Attorney General of the United States

IDA L. CASTRO,
Chairwoman, OFO, EEOC,
Respondents.

----------^----------

On Petition For A Writ Of Certiorari
To The United States Court of Appeals
for the Fourth Circuit

----------^----------

PETITION FOR A WRIT OF CERTIORARI

----------^----------

Phillip M. Duse, pro se
55 Spring Lake Drive
Stafford, VA 22554
540-659-2241

QUESTIONS PRESENTED

1. Whether a United States District Court judge, who did not personally or through assistants, review the plaintiff's motion identifying genuine issues for trial, e.g., Plaintiff Motion for Order Compelling Disclosure and Discovery, can legally claim in his final order:

   > "Because the facts and legal contentions are adequately presented in the materials before the Court, ..."

   and then render a summary judgment dismissing all claims as if the incontrovertible evidence in the plaintiff's motion had been considered.

2. Whether the information and exhibits contained in the plaintiff's "non-considered" motion address genuine issues for trial and disprove defendant contentions and assertions representing the basis for the aforementioned order.

3. Whether the defendants had an obligation to either verify or refute petitioner's tort claims regarding ruses and trick stratagems perpetrated by third parties, which include government entities.

4. Whether the tort activity noted at paragraph three above and identified in this suit was supported in part by the defendants, because the petitioner's travel itinerary was "top secret."

5. Whether the legal options and the constitutional rights of the petitioner were substantially prejudiced by the dismissal action of the district court and by the dismissal action of the district court and by the appellant court, when they excluded the incontrovertible evidence provided by the petitioner — which met his burden of proof.

6. Finally, whether the defendant's false articulations and agency contrived complaint issues, identified in this suit and proven false in briefs, should be permitted to stand as truthful with no admonishment or other corrective action by fact-finders or the court(s).

Phillip M. Duse

MOTION TO DIRECT THE CLERK TO FILE
PETITION FOR CERTIORARI OUT OF TIME

TO: Office Of The Clerk   December 5, 2000

CASE NO.   00-1437/CA-99-1400-A

     My name is Phillip M. Duse. I am the petitioner in case number 00-1437, CA-99-1400-A. My petition for writ of certiorari was returned yesterday, December 4, 2000, with comment indicating the postmarked date, 28 November 2000 exceeded the 90 day filing time that started 29 August 2000--due date of 27 November 2000.

     Be advised that by application addressed to the Office of the Clerk of the Court, dated October 31, 2000 and received Nov 2, 2000, I requested authority (Application No. 00A427) to exceed the 30-page writ of certiorari limit. Response from the office of the clerk, identifying documentation required in the application process is dated November 6, 2000 and the response denying my request to exceed the 30 page limit is dated November 14, 2000, received 17 November 2000.

     Note that the application and court response time involved a significant number of days. More than a week's time was lost in this process which held up the printing of the petition, and ultimately resulting in the one day out of time receipt of the petition by the clerk of the court.

     Therefore: Through this motion, I respectfully request direction be given to the clerk to file my petition for certiorari out of time.

                                             Phillip M. Duse
                                             Petitioner Pro Se
                                             55 Spring Lake Drive
                                             Stafford VA 22554
                                             540-659-2241

cc Joel E. Wilson
Special Assistant United States Attorney
2100 Jamieson Avenue
Alexandria, VA 22314
Telephone: (703) 299-3700

Certificate of Service

I certify that on, 5 December 2000, I mailed a complete copy of this Motion to direct the clerk to file petition for certiorari out of time, addressed as shown below.

Joel E. Wilson
Special Assistant United States Attorney
2100 Jamieson Avenue
Alexandria, VA 22314
Telephone (703) 299-3700

._____.
Phillip M. Duse

FALSE COLOR OF AUTHORITY ?
(Government Hit-Men?)

Is It The People's Responsibility
To Denigrate Phil Duse, a law abiding citizen

Or

Should They Tell Government *Animositors

Denigration Activity Must Be Supported by:

Empirical Conclusions Based on Experience or Observation that is

Verifiable or Disprovable

And Not: Systems or Theories Based on Fruits of Mental Masturbation

[See 2004: Phil Duse Versus the Tyranny of DOD/DOJ, Xlibris]

By Phillip M. Duse Sr.
Government Victim

*Animositor: Any individual who attempts to degrade or defame another through display of ill will under the direction or hidden agenda of another—aka Government perpetrators doltish behavior.

EEOC: THE REAL DEAL
(EQUAL EMPLOYMENT OPPORTUNITY COMMISSION)

Do They Really Support Title VII OF THE 1964 CIVIL RIGTS ACT?

Hold your nose and discover:

1. The author has found them to be "players of low integrity" who permitted an agency to unilaterally alter complaints and misrepresent issues to appear as the "folly of fools."

2. He also believes they assisted others, Department of Justice, DOJ, for example, and the District Federal/Appellate Courts in avoiding agency liability for proven violations of Title VII, 1964 Civil Rights Act—how? The complete story in exquisite detail is shared for your edification.

3. Another conclusion of the author holds: They appear to have assisted the U.S. Supreme Court to not rule on the merits of issues, thus denying justice by trial under Title VII!

4. It would appear that they are among the entities who took no action, looked the other way, on a griping report involving actions of "hit men" attempting to terminate the author's life—was the Government involved? See chapter 3--Why? Who else?

BY PHILLIP M. DUSE SR.

www.ingramcontent.com/pod-product-compliance
Lightning Source LLC
Chambersburg PA
CBHW052115070526
44584CB00017B/2502